KETO DIET COOKBOOK FOR WOMEN AFTER 50

REINVIGORATE YOUR BODY AND HAVE A HEALTHIER LIFESTYLE.

100 DELICIOUS RECIPES TO LOSE WEIGHT, REGAIN YOUR METABOLISM FOR STAY HEALTHY

RITA LIPSEY
Copyright © RITA LIPSEY

Editing by Gemma Preston

2. The Ketogenic Diet Pyramid

So, you have taken into consideration how your body is changing and the nutrients that you will need as you turn 50 and older. You have also gone through the health benefits, and you feel that the Keto diet is the perfect fit for you. That is wonderful! Now is the perfect time to make the first steps towards starting the Keto diet and identifying which foods you will be eating and which you should be avoiding.

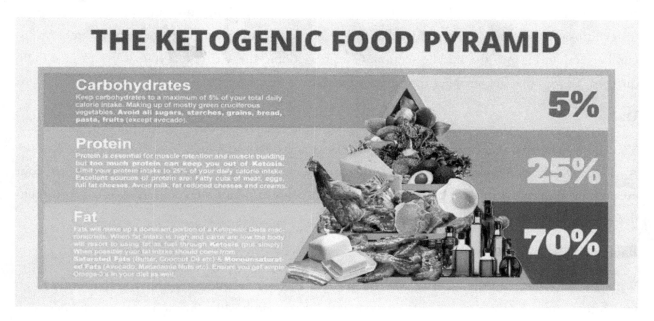

The Keto diet can appear to be quite complicated and possibly daunting at first glance when you see all the foods you can eat and which you should not. As a general rule of thumb, you should focus on increasing your consumption of healthy fatty foods, with a moderate amount of protein, while cutting out sugars and carbs.

Once you start cooking Keto, you will begin to see how easy it is, and you will quickly grasp an understanding of which foods are Keto and which are not without having to refer back to your list as frequently.

Here is the list of all of the foods that you can include in the Keto diet

These few extra foods with low amounts of carbs in them can include now and again with your meals. However, it would be best if you always moderated how much of these you eat and try to include foods containing less than 5% carbs.

Berries

When you choose berries, you should look for ones that do not contain much sugar, such as blackberries, blueberries, and raspberries. They make great snacks, but you should limit yourself to small amounts at a time because they contain sugar and carbs.

Beverages

There are a few different beverages that you can include on the Keto diet, including bone broth, unsweetened coffee and tea, and water. If you feel like switching things up with water, you can try a water infusion. For this, you should get a fusion bottle and then cut up some lemon, lime, or cucumber and add it into the middle section. Consider adding these fruits to your water to give them different flavors that get stronger throughout the day.

Dairy

You can use high-fat dairy products to create creamy and delicious foods. You can add dairy products to your diet, including butter, cream cheese, cottage cheese, heavy cream, plain Greek yogurt, sour cream, and unprocessed hard and soft cheeses. Milk often contains sugars in it, so it is recommended that you switch your milk out for cream.

Fats and oils

With the Keto diet, healthy fats and oils will become an essential energy source for your body to go into ketosis and lose weight. 78% of your diet should contain healthy fats and oils, and the best way to incorporate them into your meals is to cook with them. fats and oils that you can use include avocado oil, butter, cocoa butter, coconut butter, coconut oil, eggs, ghee, lard, olive oil, macadamia oil, mayonnaise, MCT oil, and tallow.

Fish and seafood

Fish, shellfish, and other seafood are high in healthy fats and oils. You can include all types of fish, shellfish, and seafood into your diets, such as catfish, clams, cod, crab, halibut, lobster, mussels, oysters, salmon, scallops, snapper, trout, and tuna.

Meat

It is suggested that when you buy meat that you should choose unprocessed ones, such as bacon, chicken, ground beef, ham, lamb, pork, steak, and turkey. Consider avoiding processed meat, such as cold meats, meatballs, and sausages, as much as possible because they tend to contain hidden carbs that are added in the meat production process. If you want to eat processed meat, you should limit yourself and make sure that it has less than 5% carbs.

Nuts and seeds

Another great source of healthy fats and oils comes from unsalted nuts and seeds. They work well for snacks and as toppings on your meals. Though, it would be best if you consider moderate how many nuts you have, as they can contain carbs. You can include most nuts and seeds into your Keto diets, such as almonds, Brazil nuts, chia seeds, flaxseed, macadamia nuts, pecan nuts, pumpkin seeds, sesame seeds, and walnuts.

Herbs and spices

Some Keto-friendly herbs and spices that do not contain many carbs in them include basil, cayenne pepper, chili powder, cilantro, cinnamon, cumin, garlic powder, oregano, parsley, rosemary, and thyme.

Sweeteners

You can include sweeteners like stevia and sucralose into your tea and coffee. However, they can be unhealthy for you, and you should try limiting this as much as possible.

Vegetables

When choosing vegetables to add to your dishes, you should choose ones that grow above the ground and no starchy. These include asparagus, cauliflower, cucumber, eggplants, garlic, green beans, mushrooms, olives, onions, peppers, tomatoes, and zucchini as leafy greens like broccoli, Brussels sprouts, cabbage, kale, lettuce, and spinach.

Here is the list of the foods that you should restrict or try to avoid in your diet

When you remove these foods from your diet, your body will be able to cycle into ketosis, and you will be able to meet your weight loss goals.

If you are struggling to lose weight following the Keto diet, you may need to refer back to this list to see if any foods you are eating are included or eating too many food sources containing sugar and carbs.

Alcohol

All types of alcohol should be avoided because they contain sugar and carbohydrates. It includes beer, cider, wine, and other alcoholic drinks that have been sweetened like cocktails.

Condiments

Store-bought condiments contain sugar and should be avoided. If you would like to use flavorings, I suggest that you make them yourself using Keto recipes. This way, you know precisely what you are putting into them, and there are no added sugars like you would find in bottled condiments.

Fruits

Fruits contain high amounts of sugar in them, so they should be avoided. Most fruits should be avoided unless they have low amounts of sugar in them. It includes apples, bananas, cherries, dried fruits, fruit juices, grapefruit, grapes, mangos, melon, nectarines, oranges, peaches, pears, pineapple, and plums, smoothies made from fruit, tangerines, and watermelon.

Grains

You will get most of the carbohydrates you eat come from grains. All grains, including whole grains, should be avoided when following the Keto diet. These grains include amaranth, barley, buckwheat, bulgur, flour and corn tortillas, millet, oatmeal, oats, pumpernickel, quinoa, rice, rye, sandwich wraps, sorghum, sourdough, sprouted grains, and wheat.

Legumes

Another food group that you should avoid that is high in carbohydrates is legumes. It includes black beans, cannellini, chickpeas, kidney beans, lentils, navy beans, pinto beans, and soybeans.

Low-fat dairy

Any low-fat dairy products should be avoided, and you should swap any of these out for alternatives with higher fat content. It includes fat-free yogurt, low-fat cheese, skims milk, and skim mozzarella.

Starchy vegetables

Most vegetables are fine to eat, but others contain high amounts of carbohydrates. Like with grains and legumes, you should try to avoid eating starchy vegetables in your diet. Starchy vegetables include artichokes, butternut squash, corn, parsnips, peas, potatoes, sweet potatoes, and yams.

Sugar

All forms of sugars and sweeteners that are not stevia and sucralose should be avoided. It includes agave nectar, aspartame, cane sugar, corn syrup, honey, maple syrup, saccharin, and Splenda.

Sweet treats

Because sweet treats and baked goods often contain high sugar levels, you should avoid buying these from the store. If you are craving something sweet, you can look at a few Keto dessert recipes and make yourself a few snacks and treats according to the list of allowed Keto-friendly foods.

Tran's fats and oils

Any fats and oils that contain Tran's fats are bad for your health and should be avoided. You can swap these trans fats and oils out for the healthy fats and oils on the list of allowed foods. fats and oils that contain trans fats include canola oil, grape seed oil, margarine, peanut oil, sesame oil, soybean oil, and sunflower oil.

It would be best to remember that you are not completely cutting out foods that contain carbohydrates with the Keto diet. When you first start with the Keto diet, you should begin with eating 20 grams of carbohydrates each day to put your body into ketosis. It would be best to continue with this amount to lose weight and meet your health goals before you start introducing more carbs into your diet.

When choosing foods containing carbohydrates, you should ensure that their net carbs are less than 5 grams. It works because if you have a food item with total carbs equaling 5 grams, you check how much fiber it contains. If, for example, the food item contains 2 grams of fiber, then you will subtract that from the total carbs. In this example, your net carbs will be equal to 3 grams.

You will use the net carb amount to track how many carbs you are, including in your diet. It would be best if you did this for each food item that you will be eating that contains some carbohydrates in it until you reach your maximum daily allowance of 20 grams.

Once you are ready to bring your body out of ketosis, you can increase your carbohydrate intake to between 20 to 50 grams per day.

Recipes from Italy

1. Cheese Stuffed Mushrooms

Preparation Time: 10 minutes

Cooking Time: 15 minutes

Servings: 12

Ingredients:

- 12 large mushrooms, clean, remove stems and chopped stems finely
- 1 ½ tbsp. fresh parsley, chopped
- 4 garlic cloves, minced
- ½ cup Parmesan cheese, grated
- ¼ cup Swiss cheese, grated
- 3.5 oz. cream cheese
- 1 tbsp. olive oil
- Salt

Kitchen Equipment:

- Oven
- Baking tray
- Bowl

Directions:

1. Preheat the oven to 375 F. Toss mushrooms with olive oil and place onto a baking tray. In a bowl, combine cream cheese, chopped mushrooms stems, parsley, garlic, Parmesan cheese, Swiss cheese, and salt.

2. Stuff cream cheese mixture into the mushroom caps and arrange mushrooms on the baking tray. Bake in the preheated oven for 10-15 minutes. Serve and enjoy.

Nutrition:

- 79 calories
- 6.3g fat
- 4g protein

2. Delicious Chicken Alfredo Dip

Preparation Time: 10 minutes

Cooking Time: 20 minutes

Servings: 8

Ingredients:

- 2 cups chicken, cooked and chopped in small pieces

- 1 ½ tbsp. fresh parsley, chopped

- 1 tomato, diced

- 2 bacon slices, cooked and crumbled

- 1 ½ cups mozzarella cheese, shredded

- 1 tsp. Italian seasoning

- ½ cup Parmesan cheese, grated

- 8 oz. cream cheese, softened

- 1 ½ cups Alfredo sauce, homemade & low-carb

Kitchen Equipment:

- Oven

- Baking dish

Directions:

1. Preheat the oven to 375 F. Put some cooking spray on the baking dish and set aside. Add chicken, ½ cup mozzarella cheese, Italian seasoning, Parmesan cheese, cream cheese, and Alfredo sauce to the bowl and stir to combine.

2. Spread chicken mixture into the prepared baking dish and top with remaining mozzarella cheese. Bake in a preheated oven for 20 minutes. Top with parsley, tomatoes, and bacon. Serve and enjoy.

Nutrition:

144 calories

0.5g fat

29.3g protein

3. Zucchini Tots

Preparation Time: 10 minutes

Cooking Time: 20 minutes

Servings: 4

Ingredients:

- 5 cups zucchini grated and squeeze out all liquid
- ½ tsp. garlic powder
- ½ tsp. dried oregano
- ½ cup Parmesan cheese, grated
- ½ cup cheddar cheese, shredded
- 2 eggs, lightly beaten
- Pepper
- Salt

Kitchen Equipment:

- Oven
- Baking tray

Directions:

1. Preheat the oven to 400 F. Put some cooking spray to the baking tray and set aside. Add all ingredients into the bowl and mix until well combined.

2. Make small tots from the zucchini mixture and place onto the prepared baking tray. Bake in preheated oven for 15-20 minutes. Serve and enjoy.

Nutrition:

- 353 calories
- 23.1g fat
- 9.5g carbohydrates

4. Easy & Perfect Meatballs

Preparation Time: 10 minutes

Cooking Time: 20 minutes

Servings: 8

Ingredients:

- 1 egg, lightly beaten

- 3 garlic cloves, minced

- ½ cup mozzarella cheese, shredded

- ½ cup Parmesan cheese, grated

- 1 lb. ground beef

- Pepper

- Salt

Kitchen Equipment:

- Oven

- Baking tray

- Parchment paper

Directions:

1. Using the parchment paper line, the baking tray and preheat the oven to 400 F. Set aside. Mix all ingredients into the mixing bowl.

2. Make small balls from meat mixture and place on a prepared baking tray. Bake in a preheated oven for 20 minutes. Serve and enjoy.

Nutrition:

- 157 calories

- 6.7g fat

- 21.5g protein

5. Parmesan Chicken

Preparation Time: 10 minutes

Cooking Time: 35 minutes

Servings: 4

Ingredients:

- 1 lb. chicken breasts, skinless and boneless
- 1/2 cup Parmesan cheese, grated
- 3/4 cup mayonnaise
- 1 tsp. garlic powder
- 1/2 tsp. Italian seasoning

Kitchen Equipment:

- Oven
- Baking dish

Directions:

1. Preheat the oven to 375 F. Spray baking dish with cooking spray. Combine mayonnaise, garlic powder, poultry seasoning, and pepper.

2. Transfer chicken breasts into the prepared baking dish. Spread mayonnaise mixture over chicken then sprinkles cheese on top of chicken. Bake chicken for 35 minutes. Serve and enjoy.

Nutrition:

- 391 calories
- 23g fat
- 11g carbohydrates

6. Antipasti Skewers

Preparation Time: 10 minutes

Cooking Time: 0 minute

Servings: 6

Ingredients:

- 6 small mozzarella balls

- 1 tbsp. olive oil

- Salt to taste

- 1/8 tsp. dried oregano

- 2 roasted yellow peppers, sliced into strips and rolled

- 6 cherry tomatoes

- 6 green olives, pitted

- 6 Kalamata olives, pitted

- 2 artichoke hearts, sliced into wedges

- 6 slices salami, rolled

- 6 leaves fresh basil

Kitchen Equipment:

- Skewers

Directions:

1. Toss the mozzarella balls in olive oil. Season with salt and oregano. Thread the mozzarella balls and the rest of the ingredients into skewers. Serve in a platter.

Nutrition:

- 180 calories

- 11.8g fat

- 9.2g protein

7.Eggs Benedict Deviled Eggs

Preparation Time: 15 minutes

Cooking Time: 25 minutes

Servings: 16

Ingredients:

- 8 hardboiled eggs, sliced in half

- 1 tbsp. lemon juice

- ½ tsp. mustard powder

- 1 pack Hollandaise sauce mix, prepared according to direction in the packaging

- 1 lb. asparagus, trimmed and steamed

- 4 oz. bacon, cooked and chopped

Kitchen Equipment:

- Bowl

Directions:

1. Scoop out the egg yolks. Mix the egg yolks with lemon juice, mustard powder, and 1/3 cup of the Hollandaise sauce. Spoon the egg yolk mixture into each of the egg whites.

2. Arrange the asparagus spears on a serving plate. Top with the deviled eggs. Sprinkle remaining sauce and bacon on top.

Nutrition:

- 80 calories

- 5.3g fat

- 6.2g protein

8. Bacon, Mozzarella & Avocado

Preparation Time: 15 minutes

Cooking Time: 15 minutes

Servings: 2

Ingredients:

- 3 slices bacon

- 1 cup mozzarella cheese, shredded

- 6 eggs, beaten

- 2 tbsp. butter

- ½ avocado

- 1 oz. cheddar cheese, shredded

- Salt and pepper to taste

Kitchen Equipment:

- Pan

Directions:

1. Cook the bacon until crispy. Transfer to a plate and set aside. Place the mozzarella cheese the pan and cook until the edges have browned.

2. Cook the eggs in butter. Stuff mozzarella with scrambled eggs, bacon, and mashed avocado. Sprinkle cheese on top. Season with salt and pepper.

Nutrition:

- 645 calories

- 53.6g fat

- 35.8g protein

9. Beef & Broccoli

Preparation Time: 10 minutes

Cooking Time: 15 minutes

Servings: 2

Ingredients:

- ¼ cup coconut amino, divided
- 1 tsp. garlic, minced and divided
- 1 tsp. fresh ginger, minced and divided
- 8 oz. beef, sliced thinly
- 1 ½ tbsp. avocado oil, divided
- 2 ½ cups broccoli, sliced into florets
- ¼ cup low sodium beef stock
- ½ tsp. sesame oil
- Salt to taste
- Sesame seeds
- Green onion, chopped

Kitchen Equipment:

- Pan

Directions:

1. In a bowl, mix the one tbsp. coconut amino with half of the ginger and garlic.

2. Marinate the beef into this mixture for 1 hour. Wrap it with foil and put it in the refrigerator.

3. Put 1 tbsp. oil in a pan over medium heat. Stir in the broccoli and cook for 3 minutes. Add the remaining ginger and garlic.

4. Cook for 1 minute. Reduce heat. Cover the pan with its lid. Allow the broccoli to cook until tender then, transfer in a platter. Increase the heat and add the remaining oil.

5. Add the beef and cook for 3 minutes. Put the broccoli back. In a bowl, mix the remaining coconut amino, broth, and sesame oil. Pour into the pan. Cook until the sauce has thickened.

6. Season with salt. Garnish with sesame seeds and green onion.

Nutrition:

- 298 calories
- 10g fat
- 40g protein

10. Mushroom Frittata

Preparation Time: 10 minutes

Cooking Time: 15 minutes

Servings: 6

Ingredients:

- 2 tbsp. olive oil

- 1 cup sliced fresh mushrooms

- 1 cup shredded spinach

- 6 bacon slices, cooked and chopped

- 10 large eggs, beaten

- ½ cup crumbled goat cheese

- Sea salt

- Freshly ground black pepper

Kitchen Equipment:

- Oven

- Large oven-proof skillet

Directions:

1. Preheat the oven to 350°F. Put the large oven-proof skillet over medium-high heat and add the olive oil. Cook the mushrooms until lightly browned.

2. Mix the spinach and bacon and sauté until the greens are wilted. Stir in the eggs and cook, lifting the edges of the frittata with a spatula so uncooked egg flow underneath, for 3 to 4 minutes.

3. Topped it with crumbled goat cheese and season lightly with salt and pepper.

4. Bake until set and lightly browned, about 15 minutes. Take out the frittata from the oven, and let stand for 5 minutes.

5. Cut into 6 wedges and serve immediately.

Nutrition:

- 316 calories

- 27g fat

- 16g protein

11. One Pan Pesto Chicken and Veggies

Preparation Time: 10 minutes

Cooking Time: 35 minutes

Servings: 3

Ingredients:

- 2 tbsp. olive oil
- 1 cup cherry diced tomatoes
- ¼ cup basil pesto
- 1/3 cup sun-dried tomatoes, chopped and drained
- 1-lb. chicken thigh, bones and skinless, sliced into strips
- 1-lb. asparagus, cut in half with the ends trimmed

Kitchen Equipment:

- Large skillet

Directions:

1. Start by heating a large skillet. Put two tsp. olive oil and sliced chicken on medium heat. Season with salt and add ½ cup of the sun-dried tomatoes.

2. Cook until the chicken is cooked thoroughly. Spoon out the chicken and tomatoes and put them in a separate container.

3. Do not wash the skillet just yet. You will be using the oil there later.

4. Place the asparagus in the skillet and pour it in the pesto. Turn on the heat over medium and add the remaining sun-dried tomatoes. Sauté the asparagus for 5 to 10 minutes. Put it on a separate plate when done.

5. Put the chicken back in the skillet and pour it in pesto. Stir under medium heat for 2 minutes. You only need to reheat the chicken during this, so when done, you can serve it together with the asparagus.

Nutrition:

- 104 calories
- 8g fat
- 26g protein

12. Keto Lasagna

Preparation Time: 10 minutes

Cooking Time: 75 minutes

Servings: 4

Ingredients:

- 8 oz. block of cream cheese
- 3 large eggs
- Kosher salt
- Ground black pepper
- 2 cups of shredded mozzarella
- ½ cup of freshly grated Parmesan
- Pinch crushed red pepper flakes
- Chopped parsley for garnish

For the sauce:

- ¾ cup marinara
- 1 tbsp. tomato paste
- 1 lb. ground beef
- ½ cup of freshly grated Parmesan
- 1.5 cup of shredded mozzarella
- 1 tbsp. extra virgin olive oil
- 1 tsp. dried oregano
- 3 cloves minced garlic
- ½ cup chopped onion
- 16 oz. ricotta

Kitchen Equipment:

- Oven
- Baking tray
- Parchment paper
- Microwave
- Baking sheet
- Skillet

Directions:

1. Prepare the oven at 350 F and prepare the baking tray by lining it with parchment and cooking spray.

2. Grab a microwave-safe bowl and throw in the cream cheese, mozzarella, and Parmesan, melting them together for a few seconds in the microwave. Mix them thoroughly before adding the eggs and blending the whole thing. Season it well.

3. Transfer the mixture into the baking sheet and bake for 15 to 20 minutes.

4. While baking, grab a skillet and using medium heat, coat the surface with oil. Put in the onion and allow them to cook for 5 minutes before adding the garlic. Once you get that fragrant smell, wait 60 more seconds before adding the tomato paste onto the mixture. Make sure to stir all the items around until the onion and garlic are well-coated.

5. Add the ground beef in the skillet and cook the mixture, breaking up the meat

until it is no longer pinks in appearance. Add salt and pepper to taste. Continue cooking before setting it aside and allowing it to cool. There should be a bit of fluid remaining in the skillet – try to drain that out of the meat before proceeding with the next step.

6. Turn on the stove again, keeping the medium heat constant. Add some marinara sauce and season with pepper, red pepper flakes, and ground pepper. Stir around to evenly distribute the flavor.

7. Noodles should be ready by now from the oven. Take them out and start cutting them in half widthwise and then cut them again into 3 pieces.

8. Start layering! Use an 8-inch baking pan for this, placing 2 noodles at the bottom of the dish first and layer as you wish. Alternate the Parmesan and mozzarella shreds depending on your personal preferences.

9. Let it bake until cheese melts, and the sauce bubbles out. It should take about 30 minutes.

10. Garnish and serve.

Nutrition:

- 103 calories

- 6g fat

- 28g protein

13. Tomato Chili Chicken Tender with Fresh Basils

Preparation Time: 10 minutes

Cooking Time: 50 minutes

Servings: 5

Ingredients:

- 2 lb.s of boneless chicken thighs
- 4 tbsp. extra virgin olive oil
- 3 lemongrass
- 3 tbsp. red chili flakes
- 2 ½ tbsp. minced garlic
- 2 cups water
- ¼ cup sliced red tomatoes
- ½ cup fresh basils
- Salt and pepper

Kitchen Equipment:

- Skillet
- Saucepan

Directions:

1. Defreeze your chicken. Cut the chicken into small to medium pieces. Place the pieces in a skillet.

2. Add some minced garlic and lemongrass. Add some salt and pepper to taste. Pour water over the chicken

3. Boil the chicken till the water totally/almost totally evaporates. Take out the chicken and set it aside. Heat a saucepan and pour olive oil in.

4. Place the chicken and let it cook till it is brown. Place your tomatoes, basils, and chili flakes. Serve warm.

Nutrition:

- 109 calories
- 9g fat
- 28g protein

14. Low-Carb Lasagna

Preparation Time: 15 minutes

Cooking Time: 30 minutes

Servings: 5

Ingredients:

- 16 oz ricotta
- 8 oz block cream cheese
- 4 cups of shredded mozzarella
- 4 minced cloves of garlic
- 3 large eggs
- 2 cups of freshly grated Parmesan cheese
- 1 tbsp. extra virgin olive oil
- 1 ½ tbsp. tomato paste
- 1 ½ ground beef
- ¾ cups of marinara
- ½ white or yellow onion
- 1 tbsp. dried oregano
- Cooking spray, butter, or oil
- Pinch crushed red pepper flakes
- Chopped parsley
- Black pepper
- Kosher salt

Kitchen Equipment:

- Baking pan
- Skillet
- Oven
- Baking sheet
- Parchment paper or foil

Directions:

1. Prepare the oven at 350 F. In another bowl, put in 2 ½ cups of mozzarella, 8 oz of cheese, and 1 cup of Parmesan cheese. Put in all the eggs and mix very well. Add salt and pepper to taste.

2. Pour on the baking sheet and spread it out. Bake for 15-20 minutes till it's golden. Heat some oil in a large skillet

3. Place chopped onion and fry it until it is soft. Add the garlic after and cook for a few more minutes. Poor in tomato paste

4. Heat the mixture until it is hot enough. Add salt and pepper to taste. Pour in ground beef. Cook the mixture until the meat loses its pink color

5. Add marinara. Put in red pepper flakes. Cut noodles in 6 pieces.

6. Transfer some small amount of the sauce into a baking pan. Then, put 2 noodles at

the base. Divide the ricotta into 3. Spread one part of the ricotta over the broken noodles. Spread another part on the remaining meat and sauce which is on the top. Pour in the last part with the Parmesan cheese. Make similar layers and pour cheese at the very top.

7. Place the mix in the oven until the cheese melts and the sauce heats

8. Sprinkle parsley and cheese if you wish

Nutrition:

- 109 calories

- 31g protein

- 7g fats

15. Pesto Crackers

Preparation Time: 10 Minutes

Cooking Time: 17 minutes

Servings: 6

Ingredients:

- ½ tsp. baking powder
- Salt and black pepper to the taste
- 1 and ¼ cup of almond flour
- ¼ tsp. basil, dried
- 1 garlic clove, minced
- 2 tbsp. basil pesto
- A pinch of cayenne pepper
- 3 tbsp. ghee

Kitchen Equipment:

- Oven
- Baking sheet

Directions:

1. Combine salt, pepper, baking powder, and almond flour. Stir in the garlic, cayenne, and basil. Mix in the pesto and whisk it well.

2. Then add in the ghee and combine your dough with your finger. Place this dough on a lined baking sheet, transfer into the oven at 325 F and bake for 17 minutes.

3. Set aside to cool down, cut your crackers, and serve them as a snack. Enjoy!

Nutrition:

- 9 calories
- 0.41g protein
- 0.14g fat

16. Asparagus Frittata

Preparation Time: 10 minutes

Cooking Time: 15 minutes

Servings: 4

Ingredients:

- ¼ cup Onion, chopped

- A drizzle of olive oil

- 1 lb. Asparagus spears, cut into 1-inch pieces

- Salt and ground black pepper to taste

- 4 Eggs, whisked

- 1 cup cheddar cheese, grated

Kitchen Equipment:

Pan

Directions:

1. Heat the oil over medium heat. Mix in onions, and stir-fry for 3 minutes. Stir in asparagus and stir-fry for 6 minutes. Then add eggs and stir-fry for 3 minutes.

2. Sprinkle salt, pepper, and cheese. Place in the oven and broil for 3 minutes. Divide frittata between plates and serve.

Nutrition:

- 202 calories

- 13g fat

- 15.1g protein

17. Vegetable Cream Soup

Preparation Time: 10 minutes

Cooking Time: 35 minutes

Servings: 6

Ingredients:

- 1 lb. cauliflower florets

- 1 lb. broccoli florets

- Bunch of kale or spinach, roughly chopped

- Celery ribs, chopped

- 4 tbsp. extra-virgin olive oil

- 2 medium garlic cloves, minced

- 1 medium red onion, roughly chopped

- 10 cups of homemade low-sodium vegetable stock

- 1 cup of heavy cream (more as needed)

- 1 tsp. fine sea salt

- 1 tbsp. Dijon mustard

- 1 tbsp. fresh parsley, finely chopped

Kitchen Equipment:

- Instant pot

Directions:

1. Press the "Sauté" function on your Instant Pot and add the olive oil. Once hot, add the onions and garlic cloves. Sauté until translucent, stirring frequently.

2. Add the celery, cauliflower florets, and broccoli florets. Cook for 2 minutes, stirring frequently.

3. Add the remaining ingredients except for the heavy cream inside your Instant Pot. Close the lid and cook at high pressure for 15 minutes. When done, naturally release the tension and carefully remove the cover.

4. Puree the soup using an immersion blender. Gently stir in the heavy cream and adjust the seasoning if necessary. Serve and enjoy!

Nutrition:

- 324 calories

- 16g fat

- 34g protein

18. Italian Spaghetti Casserole

Preparation Time: 10 minutes

Cooking Time: 65 minutes

Servings: 6

Ingredients:

- 1 spaghetti squash, halved
- Salt and ground black pepper to taste
- 4 tbsp. butter
- 2 cloves garlic
- 1 cup onion
- 4 oz. tomatoes
- 4 oz. Italian salami, chopped
- ½ cup Kalamata olives, chopped
- ½ tsp. Italian seasoning
- Medium eggs
- ½ cup fresh parsley, chopped

Kitchen Equipment:

- Oven
- Baking sheet

Directions:

1. Prepare the oven at 400 F. Arrange the squash on the baking sheet. Sprinkle with salt and pepper. Add 1 tbsp. butter and place in oven—Cook for 45 minutes.

2. Meanwhile, peel and mince garlic; peel and chop the onion; core and chop tomatoes. Preheat pan on medium heat, add and melt 3 tbsp. butter.

3. Add onion, garlic, and salt, and pepper, sauté for 2 minutes, stirring occasionally. Add chopped tomatoes and chopped salami. Stir and cook for 10 minutes. Add chopped olives and Italian seasoning. Stir and cook for 2-3 minutes more.

4. Remove squash halves from the oven and scrape the flesh with a fork. Combine spaghetti squash with salami mixture in pan.

5. Shape 4 spaces in the mixture and crack an egg in each. Sprinkle with salt and pepper and place pan in the oven. Cook at 400 F until eggs are done. Top with parsley and serve.

Nutrition:

- 320 calories
- 18g fat
- 38g protein

19.   Fresh Broccoli Salad with Pancetta

Preparation Time: 10 minutes

Cooking Time: 15 minutes

Servings: 3

Ingredients:

- 150g raw broccoli

- 10 g toasted almonds, chopped

- 5g finely chopped red onion

- 2 pieces of pancetta, oven-baked *Sauce:*

- 50 g mayonnaise

- 10g mustard

- 7g reduced balsamic

Kitchen Equipment:

- Oven

Directions:

1. Bake the pancetta for 15 minutes at 160 F in an oven. Cut raw broccoli into small pieces, rinse well and dry, shake off the sieve so that no water remains. Chop the red onion as thin as possible.

2. Mix broccoli, onion, mustard, mayonnaise, and balsamic sauce in a cup.

3. Mix well. Add the almonds and mix well again. After we put the salad on a plate, we put the pancetta on top and pour a little sauce over it.

4. Enjoy your meal!

Nutrition:

- 301 calories

- 5g fiber

- 14g protein

20. Keto Salad with Chicken, Pesto, and Cherry Tomatoes

Preparation Time: 10 minutes

Cooking Time: 20 minutes

Servings: 6

Ingredients:

- 2 tbsp. finely chopped rosemary
- ½ cup olive oil
- ¼ cup apple cider vinegar
- ¼ tsp. garlic paste
- 1 tbsp. mayonnaise
- 600 g chicken fillet
- 6 cups assorted salad greens
- 10 (170g) cherry tomatoes, halved
- ½ medium avocado
- 30g chopped purple onion
- 2 tbsp. shredded Parmesan cheese
- 1 tsp. salt
- 1 tsp. pepper

Kitchen Equipment:

- Bowl
- Skillet

Directions:

1. Chop the rosemary into small pieces. Half will be used to make the dressing, while the rest will be used as the chicken seasoning.

2. Make a Keto salad dressing by mixing oil, vinegar, garlic paste, mayonnaise, and rosemary in a jar with a lid.

3. Close the jar and shake vigorously to mix all the ingredients well.

4. Put the remaining rosemary over the chicken and add a pinch of salt and pepper.

5. Preheat a skillet over medium heat, grill the chicken for about 20 minutes, and flip it over 10 minutes after starting to fry. The chicken must be well done.

6. Let the chicken cool.

7. Collect the salad on a large plate or in separate bowls with a variety of herbs, cherry tomatoes, chopped onions, and avocado.

8. Chop the chicken and put on top of the salad. Sprinkle with Parmesan cheese and mix with the dressing. You can sprinkle the salad with dietary yeast.

Nutrition:

- 338 calories
- 24.7g fat
- 23.8g protein

21. Stuffed Eggs

Preparation Time: 15 minutes

Cooking Time: 10 minutes

Servings: 12

Ingredients:

- 6 Large eggs, hardboiled, peeled and halved lengthwise

- ¼ cup Creamy mayonnaise

- ¼ Avocado, chopped

- ¼ cup Swiss cheese, shredded

- ½ tsp. Dijon mustard

- Ground black pepper

- 6 Bacon slices, cooked and chopped

Kitchen Equipment:

- Bowl

Directions:

1. Pull out the yolks and put them in a bowl. Place the whites on a plate, hollow-side up.

2. Mash the yolks with a fork and add Dijon mustard, cheese, avocado, and mayonnaise. Mix well and season yolk mixture with the black pepper.

3. Spoon the yolk mixture back into the egg white hollows and top each egg half with the chopped bacon.

4. Serve.

Nutrition:

- 85 calories

- 7g fat

- 6g protein

22. Diet Salad with Bacon and Broccoli

- **Preparation Time**: 15 minutes
- **Cooking Time**: 10 minutes
- **Servings**: 6
- **Ingredients**:
- 340g broccoli cabbage
- 6 slices fried bacon
- 1/2 medium red onion
- 5 tbsp. mayonnaise
- 1 tsp. erythritol
- 1 tbsp. apple cider vinegar

Kitchen Equipment:

- Skillet

Directions:

1. Fry the bacon in a preheated skillet, remove from heat and let cool. Place broccoli and onions in a large bowl. In a smaller bowl, whisk the mayonnaise, erythritol, and apple cider vinegar together.

2. Chop the bacon, and then add it to the broccoli. Stir the sauce well and pour it into the broccoli bowl. Stir again, spreading the dressing evenly. Enjoy your meal!

Nutrition:

- 155.5 calories
- 12.92g fat
- 5.4g protein

23. Keto Salad with Canned Tuna and Pesto Sauce

Preparation Time: 10 minutes

Cooking Time: 0 minute

Servings: 1

Ingredients:

Refueling

- 1 tbsp. olive oil
- ½ tbsp. apple cider vinegar
- Salt and pepper, to taste

Salad

- 4 large iceberg lettuce leaves
- 1 small tomato
- ½ small cucumber
- ¼ medium avocado

Tuna

- 1 can of canned tuna in oil (100 g)
- 1.5 tbsp. mayonnaise
- 1.5 tbsp. full fat Greek yogurt or mayonnaise
- 1 tbsp. pesto sauce
- 2 tsp. lemon juice
- Salt, to taste

Kitchen Equipment:

- Bowl
- **Directions**:

1. Pour the olive oil, apple cider vinegar, and some salt and pepper into a jar. Shake it well. Ready the ingredients for the salad by tearing up the lettuce leaves and placing them in a bowl. Slice the tomatoes, cucumber, and avocado then arrange on top of the salad.

2. Combine the tuna, mayonnaise, yogurt, pesto, lemon juice, and some salt. Place the tuna mix to the top of the salad, then drizzle the dressing over the top.

Nutrition:

- 604.8 calories
- 46.5 g fat
- 34.5 g protein

24. Yummy Roasted Cauliflower

Preparation Time: 15 minutes

Cooking Time: 20 minutes

Servings: 5

Ingredients:

- 4 Cauliflower florets
- 4 small garlic cloves, peeled and halved
- 2 tbsp. olive oil
- 1 tbsp. fresh lemon juice
- 1 tsp. dried thyme, crushed
- 1 tsp. dried oregano, crushed
- ½ tsp. red pepper flakes
- Salt and black pepper, to taste

Kitchen Equipment:

- Oven
- 2 large baking dishes

Directions:

1. Preheat the oven to 425 F. Brush 2 large baking dishes with butter. In a large bowl, incorporate all the ingredients and toss to coat well.

2. Divide the cauliflower mixture into the prepared baking dishes evenly and spread in a single layer. Roast for about 15-20 minutes or until the desired doneness, tossing 2 times. Remove from the oven and serve hot.

Nutrition:

- 74 calories
- 1.8g protein
- 2.3g fiber

25. Delicious Cheesecake

Preparation Time: 15 minutes

Cooking Time: 70 minutes

Servings: 8

Ingredients:

- 3 eggs
- 1/4 cup shredded coconut
- 1/2 cup coconut flour
- 1/2 cup almond flour
- 1 tsp. vanilla
- 1 tbsp. stevia
- 15.5 oz. sour cream
- 8 oz. cream cheese, softened
- 1/2 cup butter, melted

Kitchen Equipment:

- Oven
- 9-inch springform pan

Directions:

1. Start to preheat oven 150 C. Spray 9-inch springform pan with cooking spray. Set aside.

For the crust

2. In a mixing bowl, combine coconut flour, almond flour, shredded coconut, and melted butter until well combined. Transfer crust mixture into the prepared pan and spread evenly and press down with a fingertip. Place pan into the fridge to set crust.

For the cheesecake filling

3. In a large bowl, beat sour cream and cream cheese together. Add egg, vanilla, and sweetener and beat until well combined. Pour cheesecake filling evenly over crust. Situate pan in a water bath and bake for 1 hour-1 hour 20 minutes. Remove cake pan from oven and set aside to cool completely.

4. Place cake pan into the fridge for 5-6 hours. Slice and serve.

Nutrition:

- 410 calories
- 39g fat
- 7.8g protein

4. Recipes from Greece

26. Creamy Avocado Sauce

Preparation Time: 5 minutes

Cooking Time: 5 minutes

Servings: 8

Ingredients:

- 1 avocado, halved, seeded, and peeled

- 1 tbsp. fresh lemon juice

- 2 garlic cloves

- 2 tbsp. olive oil

- 3 tbsp. fresh parsley, chopped

- Pepper

- Salt

Kitchen Equipment:

- Food processor

Directions:

1. Transfer all ingredients into the food processor and process until smooth. Serve and enjoy.

Nutrition:

- 83 calories

- 8.4g fat

- 2.6g carbohydrates

27. Avocado Yogurt Dip

Preparation Time: 5 minutes

Cooking Time: 5 minutes

Servings: 4

Ingredients:

- 2 avocados

- 1 lime juice

- 3 garlic cloves, minced

- ½ cup Greek yogurt

- Pepper

- Salt

Kitchen Equipment:

- Bowl

Directions:

1. Scoop out avocado flesh using the spoon and place it in a bowl. Mash avocado flesh using the fork. Add remaining ingredients and stir to combine. Serve and enjoy.

Nutrition:

- 139 calories

- 11g fat

- 4g protein

28. Keto Macadamia Hummus

Preparation Time: 10 minutes

Cooking Time: 5 minutes

Servings: 8

Ingredients:

- 1 cup macadamia nuts
- 1 ½ tbsp. tahini
- 2 tbsp. water
- 2 tbsp. fresh lime juice
- 2 garlic cloves
- 1/8 tsp. cayenne pepper
- Pepper
- Salt

Kitchen Equipment:

- Food processor

Directions:

1. Transfer all ingredients into the food processor and process until smooth. Serve and enjoy.

Nutrition:

- 138 calories
- 14.2g fat
- 1.9g protein

29. Kale Chips

Preparation Time: 5 minutes

Cooking Time: 12 minutes

Servings: 2

Ingredients:

- 1 bunch kale, removed from the stems

- 2 tbsp. extra virgin olive oil

- 1 tbsp. garlic salt

Kitchen Equipment:

- Oven

- Baking sheet

Directions:

1. Prepare the oven at 350 F. Brush the kale with olive oil. Arrange on a baking sheet.

2. Bake for 12 minutes. Sprinkle with garlic salt.

Nutrition:

- 100 calories

- 7g fat

- 2.4g protein

30. Beef Shawarma

Preparation Time: 5 minutes

Cooking Time: 15 minutes

Servings: 4

Ingredients:

- 2 tbsp. olive oil

- 1 lb. lean ground beef

- 1 cup onion, sliced

- Salt to taste

- 3 tbsp. shawarma mix

- 3 cups cabbage, shredded

- 2 tbsp. water

- 1/4 cup parsley, chopped

Kitchen Equipment:

- Pan

Directions:

1. Put your pan over medium heat. Once the pan is hot, pour the olive oil. Add the ground beef. Mix the onion and cook for 4 minutes.

2. Season with salt and shawarma mix. Add the cabbage. Pour in the water. Cover the pan and steam for 1 minute. Garnish with parsley before serving.

Nutrition:

- 330 calories

- 15.3g fat

- 35.9g protein

31. Bacon Tomato Cups

Preparation Time: 10 minutes

Cooking Time: 20 minutes

Servings: 6

Ingredients:

- 12 bacon slices

- 2 tomatoes, diced

- 1 onion, diced

- 1 cup shredded cheddar cheese

- 1 cup mayonnaise

- 12 low carb crepes/pancakes

- 1 tsp. dried basil

- Chopped chives to garnish

Kitchen Equipment:

- Skillet

- Baking sheet

- Oven

Directions:

1. Deep-fried the bacon in a skillet over medium heat for 5 minutes. Remove and chop with a knife. Transfer to a bowl. Add in cheddar cheese, tomatoes, onion, mayonnaise, and basil. Mix well set aside.

2. Place the crepes on a flat surface and use egg rings to cut a circle out of each crepe. Brush the muffin cups with cooking spray and fit the circled crepes into them to make a cup.

3. Now, fill the cups with 3 tbsp. bacon-tomato mixture. Place the muffin cups on a baking sheet, and bake for 18 minutes. Garnish with the chives, and serve with a tomato or cheese sauce.

Nutrition:

- 425 calories

- 45.2g fat

- 16.2g protein

32. Breakfast Bake

Preparation Time: 10 minutes

Cooking Time: 50 minutes

Servings: 8

Ingredients:

- 1 tbsp. olive oil
- 1-lb. sausage
- 8 large eggs
- 2 cups cooked spaghetti squash
- 1 tbsp. chopped fresh oregano
- Sea salt
- Freshly ground black pepper
- ½ cup shredded cheddar cheese

Kitchen Equipment:

- 9x13 casserole dish
- Oven
- Large oven-proof skillet

Directions:

1. Preheat the oven to 375. Brush the 9-by-13-inch casserole dish with olive oil and set aside. Place a large oven-proof skillet over medium-heat and add the olive oil.

2. Brown the sausage until cooked through, about 5 minutes. While the sausage is cooking, whisk together the eggs, squash, and oregano in a medium bowl. Season lightly and set aside.

3. Mix the cooked sausage to the egg mixture, stir until just combined, and pour the mixture into the casserole dish.

4. Sprinkle the top of the casserole with the cheese and cover the casserole loosely with aluminum foil.

5. Bake the casserole for 30 minutes, and then remove the foil and bake for another 15 minutes.

6. Let it rest first before serving.

Nutrition:

- 303 calories
- 24g fat
- 17g protein

33. Keto Pancakes

Preparation Time: 5 minutes

Cooking Time: 5 minutes

Servings: 12

Ingredients:

- 3 tbsp. coconut flour
- 3 tbsp. sour cream
- ¼ cup butter softened
- 4 eggs
- 1 tsp. baking powder
- 1 tsp. vanilla extract
- 1 tbsp. powdered sweetener
- ¼ cup water

Kitchen Equipment:

- Medium-sized bowl
- Large bowl
- Hand mixer
- Non-stick skillet

Directions:

1. Incorporate all dry ingredients in a medium-sized bowl. Mix well and set aside. In a large mixing bowl, combine sour cream with butter, vanilla extract, and water. Mix on high for 2 minutes. Add eggs, one at a time, beating constantly.

2. Add dry ingredients and continue to mix for 3 minutes. Grease a non-stick skillet with oil and heat over medium-high heat.

Using a large spoon, pour batter into skillet and cook for 2 minutes or until bubbles disappear. Flip and continue to cook for one more minute.

3. Serve immediately.

Nutrition:

- 78 calories
- 2.5g protein
- 1.5g carbs

34. Artichoke Omelet

Preparation Time: 10 minutes

Cooking Time: 10 minutes

Servings: 4

Ingredients:

- 6 eggs, beaten
- 2 tbsp. heavy (whipping) cream
- 8 bacon slices, cooked and chopped
- 1 tbsp. olive oil
- ¼ cup chopped onion
- ½ cup chopped artichoke hearts (canned, packed in water)
- Sea Salt
- Freshly ground black pepper

Kitchen Equipment:

- Small bowl
- Large skillet

Directions:

1. Beat together the eggs, heavy cream, and bacon until well blended and set aside. Put the large skillet over medium-high heat and add the olive oil.

2. Sauté the onion until tender, about 3 minutes. Pour the mixture into the skillet, swirling it for 1 minute.

3. Cook the omelet, lifting the edges with a spatula to let the uncooked egg flow underneath, for 2 minutes. Sprinkle the artichoke hearts on top and flip the omelet. Cook for 4 minutes more, until the egg is firm. Flip the omelet over again so the artichoke hearts area on top.

4. Remove from the heat, cut the omelet into quarters, and season with salt and black pepper. Serve while hot.

Nutrition:

- 435 calories
- 39g fat
- 17g protein

35. Basic Bulletproof Coffee Drink

Preparation Time: 2 minutes

Cooking Time: 1 minute

Servings: 1

Ingredients:

- 1 cup brewed coffee

- 1 tsp. coconut oil

- 1 tbsp. butter, unsalted

- ¼ tsp. vanilla extract

- A few drops of stevia

Kitchen Equipment:

- Blender

Directions:

1. Put all ingredients into a blender. Combine until frothy. Drink immediately.

Nutrition:

- 148 calories

- 14g fat

36. Keto Butter Chicken

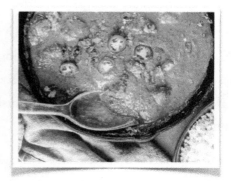

Preparation Time: 10 minutes

Cooking Time: 35 minutes

Servings: 4

Ingredients:

- 1.5 lb. chicken breast
- 1 tbsp. coconut oil
- 2 tbsp. garam masala
- 3 tsp. grated fresh ginger
- 3 tsp. minced garlic
- 4 oz. plain yogurt

For the sauce:

- 2 tbsp. butter
- 1 tbsp. ground coriander
- ½ cup heavy cream
- ½ tbsp. garam masala
- 2 tsp. fresh ginger, grated
- 2 tsp. minced garlic
- 2 tsp. cumin
- 1 tsp. chili powder
- 1 onion
- 14.5 oz. crushed tomatoes
- Salt to taste

Kitchen Equipment:

- Large bowl
- Blender

Directions:

1. Start by cutting the chicken into pieces measuring around 2 inches each. Place it in a large Bowl and add 2 tbsp. garam masala, 1 tsp. minced garlic, and 1 tsp. grated ginger. Stir slowly and add the yogurt. Make sure that mix is evenly distributed before putting a lid on the container and chilling it in the fridge for 30 minutes.

2. For the sauce, grab a blender and put in the ginger, garlic, onion, tomatoes, and spices. Blend until smooth.

3. Leave the blended sauce aside and grab a skillet. Thaw the chicken and cook on medium heat, allowing it to brown on both sides.

4. Once cooked, pour in the sauce, and allow it to simmer for 5 more minutes

5. Finally, put in the cream and ghee, still using medium heat. Add some salt for taste and serve!

Nutrition:

- 105 calories
- 4g fat
- 19g fiber

37. Creamy Tuscan Garlic Chicken

Preparation Time: 10 minutes

Cooking Time: 30 minutes

Servings: 4

Ingredients:

- 1.5 lb. boneless and skinless chicken breast

- ½ cup chicken broth

- ½ cup Parmesan cheese

- ½ cup sun dried tomatoes

- 1 cup heavy cream

- 1 cup chopped spinach

- 2 tbsp. olive oil

- 1 tsp. garlic powder

- 1 tsp. Italian seasoning

Kitchen Equipment:

- Large skillet

Directions:

1. Grab a large skillet and cook the chicken using olive oil using medium heat. Do this for 5 minutes for each side or until they are thoroughly cooked. Set it aside in a plate.

2. Using the same skillet, combine the heavy cream, garlic powder, Italian seasoning, Parmesan cheese, and chicken broth. Expose it to medium heat and just whisk away until the mixture thickens.

3. Add the sundried tomatoes and spinach and let it simmer until the spinach wilts.

4. Add the chicken back and serve.

Nutrition:

- **107 calories - 9g fat - 27g protein**

38. Lemony Chicken Drumsticks

Preparation Time: 15 minutes

Cooking Time: 40 minutes

Servings: 6

Ingredients

- 3 lb. grass-fed chicken drumsticks
- ½ cup butter, melted
- ¼ cup fresh lemon juice
- 2 tsp. garlic, minced
- 2 tsp. Italian seasoning
- Salt and ground white pepper, to taste

Kitchen Equipment:

- Large mixing bowl
- Oven
- Baking sheet

Directions:

1. Add butter, lemon juice, garlic, Italian seasoning, salt, and black pepper in a large mixing bowl and mix well. Stir in the chicken drumsticks and coat with the marinade generously.

2. Cover the bowl and refrigerate for at least 3–5 hours. Preheat the oven to 400 F. Grease a large baking sheet.

3. Arrange the drumsticks onto the prepared baking sheet in a single layer. Bake for approximately 40 minutes or until desired doneness. Serve hot.

Nutrition:

- 528 calories
- 28.8g fat
- 62.7g protein

39. Chicken with Capers Sauce

Preparation Time: 15 minutes

Cooking Time: 22 minutes

Servings: 2

Ingredients:

- 2 (5½ oz.) grass-fed boneless, skinless chicken thighs cut in half horizontally
- Salt and ground black pepper, to taste
- 1/3 cup almond flour
- 2 tbsp. Parmesan cheese, shredded
- ½ tsp. garlic powder
- 4 tbsp. olive oil
- 1 tbsp. garlic, minced
- 3 tbsp. capers
- ¼ tsp. red pepper flakes, crushed
- 3–4 tbsp. fresh lemon juice
- 1 cup homemade chicken broth
- 1/3 cup heavy cream

Kitchen Equipment:

- Shallow dish
- Large wok

Directions:

1. Rub chicken breast with salt and pepper. In a low dish, put the flour, Parmesan cheese, and garlic powder and mix well.

2. Coat the chicken breasts with the breading, shaking off any excess. Cook the oil in a large wok over medium-high heat and cook the chicken thighs on both side.

3. With a slotted spoon, situate the chicken thighs onto a plate then wrap it with foil keep warm. Remove the oil from the wok, leaving 1 tbsp.. Stir in the capers, garlic, red pepper flakes, lemon juice, and broth, and beat until well combined.

4. In the same pan, stir in the capers mixture over medium heat and remove the brown bits at the bottom. Cook until desired thickness, stirring occasionally. Pull out from the heat and pour in the heavy cream until smooth.

5. Again, place the wok over medium heat and continue cooking for about 1 minute. Place the cooked chicken and remove from the heat. Serve immediately.

Nutrition:

- 783 calories
- 59.4g fat
- 50.7g protein

40. Lemony Chicken Thighs

Preparation Time: 10 minutes

Cooking Time: 16 minutes

Servings: 4

Ingredients

- 2 tbsp. olive oil, divided
- 1 tbsp. fresh lemon juice
- 1 tbsp. lemon zest, grated
- 2 tsp. dried oregano
- 1 tsp. dried thyme
- Salt and ground black pepper, to taste
- 1½ lb. grass-fed bone-in chicken thighs

Kitchen Equipment:

- Oven
- Oven-proof wok

Directions:

1. Preheat the oven to 420 F. Add 1 tbsp. the oil, lemon juice, lemon zest, dried herbs, salt, and black pepper in a large mixing bowl and mix well.

2. Add the chicken thighs and coat with the mixture generously. Refrigerate to marinate for at least 20 minutes. In an oven-proof wok, heat the remaining oil over medium-high heat and sear the chicken thighs for about 2–3 minutes per side.

3. Immediately, transfer the wok into the oven and bake for approximately 10 minutes. Serve hot.

Nutrition:

- 388 calories
- 19.7g fat
- 49.4g protein

41. Grilled Pork Chops

Preparation Time: 10 minutes

Cooking Time: 12 minutes

Servings: 4

Ingredients:

- ¼ cup fresh basil leaves, minced

- 2 garlic cloves, minced

- 2 tbsp. butter, melted

- 2 tbsp. fresh lemon juice

- Salt and ground black pepper, as required

- 4 (6- to 8-oz.) bone-in pork loin chops

Kitchen Equipment:

- grill

- baking dish

Directions:

1. In a baking dish, add the basil, garlic, butter, lemon juice, salt, and black pepper, and mix well. Add the chops and generously coat with the mixture. Cover the baking dish and refrigerate for about 30–45 minutes.

2. Preheat a gas grill to medium-high heat. Lightly, grease the grill grate. Place chops onto the grill and cook for about 6 minutes per side or until desired doneness. Serve hot.

Nutrition:

- 600 calories

- 48g fat

- 38.5g protein

42. Salad of Prawns and Mixed Lettuce Greens

Preparation Time: 10 minutes

Cooking Time: 15 minutes

Servings: 3

Ingredients:

- 2 cups mixed lettuce greens
- ¼ cup aioli
- 1 tbsp. olive oil
- ½ lb. tiger prawns, peeled and deveined
- ½ tsp. Dijon mustard
- Salt and chili pepper to season
- 1 tbsp. lemon juice

Kitchen Equipment:

- Frying pan
- Small bowl

Directions:

- Season the prawns with salt and chili pepper. Fry in warm olive oil over medium heat for 3 minutes on each side until prawns are pink. Set aside. Add the aioli, lemon juice and mustard in a small bowl. Mix until smooth and creamy.
- Place the mixed lettuce greens in a bowl and pour half of the dressing on the salad. Toss with 2 spoons until mixed, and add the remaining dressing. Divide salad among plates and serve with prawns.

Nutrition:

- 107 calories
- 4g fat
- 26g protein

43. Tuna Pickle Boats

Preparation Time: 40 minutes

Cooking Time: 0 minute

Servings: 4

Ingredients:

- 1 (5-oz) can tuna, drained
- 2 large dill pickles
- ¼ tsp. lemon juice
- 2 tsp. mayonnaise
- ¼ tbsp. onion flakes
- 1 tsp. dill. chopped

Kitchen Equipment:

- Bowl

Directions:

1. Cut the pickles in half lengthwise. With a spoon, scarpe out the seeds to create boats; set aside.

2. Combine the mayonnaise, tuna, onion flakes, and lemon juice in a bowl. Fill each boat with tuna mixture. Sprinkle with dill and place in the fridge for 30 minutes before serving.

Nutrition:

- 118 calories
- 10g fat
- 34g protein

44. Green Chili Chicken Soup

Preparation Time: 10 minutes

Cooking Time: 40 minutes

Servings: 6

Ingredients:

- 3 boneless, skinless chicken breasts

- red bell pepper, seeds removed and chopped

- 2 tbsp. coconut oil, melted

- breasts and sear on both sides until brown.

- Gently stir in the remaining ingredients. Close and cook on high pressure for 15 minutes. When done, let full natural release method. Carefully remove the cover.

- Transfer chicken to a cutting board and shred using two forks. Stir the shredded chicken into the soup and adjust the seasoning if necessary. Serve and enjoy!

Nutrition:

- 314 calories

- 16g fat

- 39g protein

45. Egg Drop Soup

Preparation Time: 10 minutes

Cooking Time: 15 minutes

Servings: 4

Ingredients:

- 2 cups homemade low-sodium chicken stock
- 3 large organic eggs, beaten
- 3 fresh scallions, chopped
- 1 tbsp. fresh ginger, minced
- 1 tsp. toasted sesame oil
- 1 tsp. garlic powder
- 1 tsp. fine sea salt
- 1 tsp. freshly black pepper
- 1 tsp. xanthan gum
- A drop of yellow food coloring.

Kitchen Equipment:

- Instant pot

Directions:

1. Add all the ingredients inside your Instant Pot except for the arrowroot powder and give a good stir.

2. Close the lid and cook at high pressure for few minutes. Once done, naturally release the tension and carefully remove the cover. Stir in the yellow food coloring and arrowroot powder.

3. Cook until the liquid thickens, stirring occasionally. Serve and enjoy!

Nutrition:

- 320 calories
- 15g fat
- 37g protein

46. Lamb and Herb Bone Broth

Preparation Time: 10 minutes

Cooking Time: 80 minutes

Servings: 8

Ingredients:

- 1 lb. of lamb bones

- 1 large onion, quartered

- 3 medium carrots, cut into chunks

- 3 celery stalks, roughly chopped

- 2 whole garlic cloves

- 2 fresh sprigs of rosemary

- 2 fresh sprigs of thyme

- 8 cups of water

Kitchen Equipment:

- Instant pot

- Mason jars

Directions:

1. Add all the ingredients inside your Instant Pot. Close lid and cook at high pressure for 50 minutes. When the cooking is done, naturally release the tension and remove the cover.

2. Strain the liquid through a fine-mesh strainer. Transfer the cash to mason jars. Refrigerate and use as needed.

Nutrition:

- 320 calories

- 14g fat

- 38g protein

47. Bok Choy and Turkey Soup

Preparation Time: 10 minutes

Cooking Time: 40 minutes

Servings: 8

Ingredients:

- 1/2 lb. baby Bok choy, sliced into quarters lengthwise
- 2 lb. turkey carcass
- 1 tbsp. olive oil
- 1/2 cup leeks, chopped
- 1 celery rib, chopped
- 3 carrots, sliced
- 6 cups turkey stock
- Himalayan salt and black pepper, to taste

Kitchen Equipment:

- Heavy-bottomed pot

Directions:

1. In a heavy-bottomed pot, heat olive oil. Once hot, sauté the celery, carrots, leek, and Bok choy for about 6 minutes. Add the salt, pepper, turkey, and stock; bring to a boil.

2. Turn the heat to simmer. Continue to cook, partially covered, for about 35 minutes.

Nutrition:

- 312 calories
- 18g fat
- 31g protein

48. Delicious Ricotta Cake

Preparation Time: 10 minutes

Cooking Time: 45 minutes

Servings: 8

Ingredients:

- 2 eggs

- ½ cup erythritol

- ¼ cup coconut flour

- 15 oz. ricotta

- Pinch of salt

Kitchen Equipment:

- Oven

- 9-inch baking pan

Directions:

1. Start oven then preheats to 350 F/ 180C. Spray 9-inch baking pan with cooking spray and set aside. In a bowl whisk egg. Combine all ingredients.

2. Transfer batter in prepared baking pan. Bake in a preheated oven for 45 minutes. Remove baking pan from the oven and allow cooling completely. Slice and serve.

Nutrition:

- 91 calories

- 2.9g carbs

- 3g protein

49. Vanilla Butter Cake

Preparation Time: 10 minutes

Cooking Time: 35 minutes

Servings: 9

Ingredients:

- 5 eggs
- 1 tsp. baking powder
- 1 Oz. almond flour
- 1/2 cup butter, softened
- 1 cup Swerve
- 4 oz. cream cheese, softened
- 1 tsp. vanilla
- 1 tsp. orange extract

Kitchen Equipment:

- Oven
- 9-inch cake pan

Directions:

1. Preheat oven at 350 F/ 180C. Grease 9-inch cake pan with cooking spray and set aside. Add all ingredients into the mixing bowl and whisk until batter is fluffy. Bake for 35-40 minutes. Slices and serve.

Nutrition:

- 289 calories
- 27.2g fat
- 2.2g fiber

50. Chicken Piccata

Preparation Time: 15 minutes

Cooking Time: 22 minutes

Servings: 2

Ingredients:

- 2 (5½-oz) grass-fed boneless, skinless chicken thighs, cut in half horizontally
- Salt and ground black pepper, to taste
- 1/3 cup almond flour
- ½ tsp. garlic powder
- 2 tbsp. Parmesan cheese, shredded
- 4 tbsp. olive oil
- 1 tbsp. garlic, minced
- 3 tbsp. capers
- ¼ tsp. red pepper flakes, crushed
- 3–4 tbsp. fresh lemon juice
- 1 cup homemade chicken broth
- 1/3 cup heavy cream

Kitchen Equipment:

- Shallow dish
- Large wok

Directions:

1. Season well the chicken breasts. In a deep dish, place the flour, Parmesan cheese and garlic powder and mix well.

2. Coat the chicken breasts with the flour mixture, brush off any excess. Pour the oil in a wok over medium-high heat and cook the chicken thighs each side.

3. With a slotted spoon, transfer the chicken thighs onto a platter, and seal it with foil to remain hot. Remove the oil from the wok, leaving 1 tbsp. Combine the capers, garlic, red pepper flakes, lemon juice, and broth.

4. Mix in the capers mixture over medium heat and take out the brown bits from the bottom of the pan. Cook until desired thickness, stirring infrequently. Take it out from heat and put in the heavy cream until smooth.

5. Again, place the wok over medium heat and cook for a minute. Mix the cooked chicken and remove from the heat. Serve immediately.

Nutrition:

- 783 calories
- 59.4g fat
- 50.7g protein

5. Recipes from France

51. Beef Stroganoff

Preparation Time: 20 minutes

Cooking Time: 70 minutes

Servings: 10

Ingredients:

- ¼ cup avocado oil
- 1 white onion, chopped
- 2 tsp. garlic, minced
- 3 lb. beef brisket, fat trimmed and sliced into bite-size pieces
- Salt and pepper to taste
- 2 tsp. ground thyme
- 1 ½ cups beef broth
- 2 tbsp. apple cider vinegar
- 16 oz. fresh mushrooms, sliced
- ¾ cup sour cream
- ¼ cup mayonnaise
- 1 ½ tsp. xanthan gum

Kitchen Equipment:

- Pan

Directions:

1. Place your pan over medium heat. Add the oil, onion and garlic. Sauté for 3 minutes. Add the beef. Season with salt, pepper and thyme. Cook for 8 minutes, stirring frequently.

2. Reduce heat and add beef broth and vinegar. Simmer for 30 minutes. Add mushrooms and cover the pan. Simmer for 1 hour and 30 minutes. Remove the pan from the stove.

3. Stir in the mayonnaise and sour cream. Gradually stir in the xanthan gum until the sauce has thickened. Close the pan and let sit for 10 minutes before serving.

Nutrition:

- 343 calories
- 15.1g fat
- 44.4g protein

52. Low-Carb Crepe

Preparation Time: 5 minutes

Cooking Time: 10 minutes

Servings: 2

Ingredients:

- Batter

- 2 oz. cream cheese (full fat)

- 2 eggs

Topping

- ½ cup mixed berries

- 2 tsp. heavy whipping cream

Kitchen Equipment:

- Microwave

- Hand mixer

Directions:

1. Melt cream cheese in a microwave. Mix 2 eggs simultaneously to cream cheese and mix well using hand blender. Stir in any spices to the mixture if desired. Heat up the skillet, slightly pour some oil and make your crepes.

Nutrition:

- 162 calories

- 14.2g fat

- 7.7g protein

53. Roasted Chicken

Preparation Time: 15 minutes

Cooking Time: 70 minutes

Servings: 5

Ingredients:

- 3 tbsp. olive oil
- 3 garlic cloves, minced
- 2 tsp. fresh lime zest, grated
- 2 tsp. dried rosemary, crushed
- Salt and ground black pepper, to taste
- 1 (3-lb.) grass-fed frying chicken, neck and giblets removed

Kitchen Equipment:

- Large bowl
- Oven
- Roasting pan

Directions:

1. Combine all the ingredients except the chicken well. Add the chicken and coat with the mixture generously. Refrigerate to marinate overnight, turning occasionally.

2. Preheat the oven to 425°F. Remove the chicken from the bowl and arrange in a roasting pan. Coat the chicken with marinade.

3. With a kitchen string, tie the legs and tuck the wings back under the body. Roast for about 10 minutes.

4. Now, adjust the temperature of the oven to 350°F. and roast for about 1½ hours. Remove the roasting pan from oven and place the chicken onto a cutting board for about 10 minutes before carving.

5. Slice the chicken into desired-sized pieces and serve.

Nutrition:

- 594 calories
- 1g carbs
- 78.9g protein

54. Stuffed Chicken Breasts

Preparation Time: 15 minutes

Cooking Time: 30 minutes

Servings: 4

Ingredients:

- 1 tsp. paprika
- ¼ tsp. onion powder
- ¼ tsp. garlic powder
- Salt, to taste
- 4 grass-fed chicken breasts
- 1 tbsp. olive oil
- 4 oz cream cheese, softened
- ¼ cup Parmesan cheese, grated
- 2 tbsp. mayonnaise
- 1½ cups fresh spinach, chopped
- 1 tsp. garlic, minced
- ½ tsp. red pepper flakes, crushed

Kitchen Equipment:

- Oven
- Small bowl
- 9x13 baking dish

Directions:

1. Preheat the oven to 375°F. Combine together spices and salt. Situate the chicken breasts onto a cutting board and drizzle with oil.

2. Now, rub the chicken breasts with spice mixture evenly. With a sharp knife, cut a pocket into the side of each chicken breast. Place cream cheese, Parmesan, mayonnaise, spinach, garlic, red pepper, and ½ tsp. salt in a small mixing bowl and mix until well combined.

3. Stuff each chicken pocket with spinach mixture evenly. Arrange the chicken breasts into a 9x13-inch baking dish. Bake for about 25–30 minutes or until chicken is done completely. Serve hot.

Nutrition:

- 468 calories
- 30.2g fat
- 45.7g protein

55. Herbed Lamb Chops

Preparation Time: 10 minutes

Cooking Time: 20 minutes

Servings: 4

Ingredients:

- 1½ lb.s grass-fed lamb loin chops, trimmed

- 1 tbsp. fresh lemon juice

- ¼ cup fresh parsley, chopped

- 2 tbsp. fresh mint leaves, chopped

- 1 tbsp. olive oil

- Salt and ground black pepper, to taste

Kitchen Equipment:

- Grill

Directions:

1. Preheat grill to medium-high heat. Grease the grill grate. In a bowl, add lamb loin chops, lemon juice, parsley, mint, oil, salt, and black pepper and mix well.

2. Situate the chops onto the grill and cook for about 10 minutes per side or until desired doneness. Serve hot.

Nutrition:

- 350 calories

- 16.1g fat

- 48g protein

56. Stuffed Leg of Lamb

Preparation Time: 20 minutes

Cooking Time: 70 minutes

Servings: 14

Ingredients:

- 4 tsp. olive oil, divided
- ¼ cup scallions, chopped
- 2 garlic cloves, chopped finely
- 1 cup fresh spinach leaves, shredded
- 2 tbsp. sun-dried tomatoes (in olive oil)
- ¼ cup fresh basil leaves, shredded
- 2 tbsp. pine nuts
- 2 tsp. lemon pepper, divided
- ½ cup feta cheese, crumbled
- 1 (4-5-lb.) grass-fed boneless leg of lamb, trimmed and butterflied

Kitchen Equipment:

- Oven
- Roasting pan
- Medium wok
- Aluminum foil

Directions:

1. Preheat the oven to 325 F. Arrange a greased rack into a roasting pan.

2. In a medium wok, heat 2 tsp. the olive oil over medium heat and sauté the scallion and garlic for about 2 minutes.

3. Stir in the spinach, sun-dried tomatoes, basil, pine nuts, and 1 tsp. the lemon pepper and cook for about 2–3 minutes, stirring frequently.

4. Take out from heat and stir in feta cheese. Set aside. Remove the strings from the leg of the lamb and open it. Place the stuffing in the center of meat evenly and roll to seal the filling.

5. Carefully, tie the leg of lamb with kitchen string. Coat the rolled leg of lamb with the remaining oil and sprinkle with 1 tsp. lemon pepper. Arrange the rolled leg of lamb into the prepared roasting pan.

6. Roast for about 2 hours. Remove the leg of lamb from the oven and place onto a cutting board.

7. With a piece of foil, cover the leg of lamb for 10 minutes before slicing. Cut into desired-sized slices and serve.

Nutrition:

- 340 calories
- 15.3g fat
- 46.6g protein

57. Pork Chops in Cream Sauce

Preparation Time: 15 minutes

Cooking Time: 35 minutes

Servings: 4

Ingredients:

- 2 tbsp. olive oil
- 4 large boneless rib pork chops
- Salt, to taste
- 3 tbsp. yellow onion, chopped finely
- 2 tbsp. fresh rosemary, chopped
- 1/3 cup homemade chicken broth
- 1 tbsp. Dijon mustard
- 1 tbsp. unsalted butter
- 2/3 cup heavy cream
- 2 tbsp. sour cream
- 2 tbsp. fresh parsley, minced

Kitchen Equipment:

- Large wok

Directions

1. Cook the oil in a large wok over medium heat and sear the chops with the salt for about 3–4 minutes or until browned completely. With a slotted spoon, transfer the pork chops onto a plate and set aside.

2. Place the mushrooms, onion, and rosemary, and sauté for about 3 minutes. Stir it in the cooked chops, broth and bring to a boil.

3. Lower the heat. Cover for about 20 minutes. With a slotted spoon, transfer the pork chops onto a plate and set aside.

4. In the wok, add the butter, heavy cream, and sour cream, and stir until smooth. Stir in the cooked pork chops and cook for about 2–3 minutes or until heated completely. Serve hot.

Nutrition:

- 727 calories
- 61.4g fat
- 39.6g protein

58. Scrambled Eggs with Buttered Basil

Preparation Time: 5 minutes

Cooking Time: 15 minutes

Servings: 2

Ingredients:

- 2 oz butter

- 4 eggs

- 4 tbsp. coconut cream or coconut milk or sour cream

- 4 tbsp. fresh basil

- Salt to taste

Kitchen Equipment:

- Non-stick pan

- Small bowl

Directions:

1. Place a non-stick pan on low heat and melt butter. In a small bowl, whisk eggs, coconut cream, basil and salt. Pour into the hot pan. With a spatula, stir eggs until scrambled and cooked to desired doneness. Serve warm, or place in meal prep container to save for later.

Nutrition:

- 427 calories

- 42g fat

- 13g protein

59. Tasty Onion and Cauliflower Dip

Preparation Time: 60 minutes

Cooking Time: 30 minutes

Servings: 24

Ingredients:

- 1 and ½ cups chicken stock
- 1 cauliflower head, florets separated
- ¼ cup mayonnaise
- ½ cup yellow onion, chopped
- ¾ cup cream cheese
- ½ tsp. chili powder
- ½ tsp. cumin, ground
- ½ tsp. garlic powder
- Salt and black pepper to the taste

Kitchen Equipment:

- Pot
- Immersion blender

Directions:

1. Put the stock in a pot, add cauliflower and onion, heat up over medium heat and cook for 30 minutes. Add chili powder, salt, pepper, cumin and garlic powder and stir.

2. Also add cream cheese and stir a bit until it melts. Blend using an immersion blender and mix with the mayo. Place it in a bowl and store in the fridge for 2 hours before you serve it. Enjoy!

Nutrition:

- 40 calories
- 1.23g protein
- 3.31g fat

60. Taco Flavored Cheddar Crisps

Preparation Time: 20 minutes

Cooking Time: 15 minutes

Servings: 6

Ingredients:

- ¾ c sharp cheddar cheese, finely shredded

- ¼ c Parmesan cheese, finely shredded

- ¼ t chili powder

- ¼ t ground cumin

Kitchen Equipment:

- Oven

- Cookie sheet

- Parchment paper

Directions:

1. Preheat the oven to 400 F. Line cookie sheet with parchment paper. In a bowl, incorporate all ingredients together until well mixed. Make 12 piles of cheese parchment paper.

2. Press down the cheese into a thin layer of cheese. Bake for 5 minutes until cheese if bubby. Allow cooling on parchment paper.

3. When completely cool, peel the paper away from the crisps. These are a good Keto substitute for chips. They are cheesy and crisp. Enjoy!

Nutrition:

- 13 calories

- 1.36g protein

- 0.2g fat

61. Keto Seed Crispy Crackers

Preparation Time: 35 minutes

Cooking Time: 55 minutes

Servings: 30

Ingredients:

- 1/3 cup almond flour
- 1/3 cup sunflower seed kernels
- 1/3 cup pumpkin seed kernels
- 1/3 cup flaxseed
- 1/3 cup chia seeds
- 1 tbsp. ground psyllium husk powder
- 1 tsp. salt
- ¼ cup melted coconut oil
- 1 cup boiling water

Kitchen Equipment:

- Oven
- Parchment paper

Directions:

1. Preheat the oven to 300 F. Incorporate all dry ingredients together in a medium-sized bowl until thoroughly mixed. Add coconut oil and boiling water to dry ingredients and stir until all ingredients are mixed well.

2. On a flat surface, roll the dough between two pieces of parchment paper until approximately 1/8 inch thick. Slide the dough, still between parchment paper onto a baking sheet.

3. Pull out the top layer of parchment paper and place dough on a baking sheet into the oven. Bake 40 minutes until golden brown.

4. Score the top of the dough into cracker sized pieces. Leave in the oven to cool down. When the big cracker is cool, break into pieces.

Nutrition:

- 61 calories:
- 1g carbohydrates
- 2g protein

62. Parmesan Crackers

Preparation Time: 10 minutes

Cooking Time: 5 minutes

Servings: 8

Ingredients:

- 1 tsp. Butter

- 8 oz. Full-fat Parmesan, shredded

Kitchen Equipment:

- Oven

- Baking sheet

- Parchment paper

Directions:

1. Preheat the oven to 400 F. Set the parchment paper on the baking sheet and lightly grease the paper with the butter. Spoon the Parmesan cheese onto the baking sheet in mounds, spread evenly apart.

2. Spread out the mounds with the back of a spoon until they are flat.

3. Bake about 5 minutes, or until the center are still pale, and edges are browned. Remove, cool, and serve.

Nutrition:

- 133 calories

- 11g fat

- 11g protein

63. Almond Garlic Crackers

Preparation Time: 10 minutes

Cooking Time: 15 minutes

Servings: 4

Ingredients:

- ½ cup Almond flour

- ½ cup Ground flaxseed

- 1/3 cup Shredded Parmesan cheese

- 1 tsp. Garlic powder

- ½ tsp. Salt

- Water as needed

Kitchen Equipment:

- Baking sheet

- Parchment paper

- Oven

Directions:

1. Set the parchment paper into the baking sheet and preheat the oven to 400F. In a bowl, mix salt, Parmesan cheese, garlic powder, water, ground flaxseed, and almond meal. Set aside for 3 to 5 minutes.

2. Put dough on the baking sheet and cover with plastic wrap. Flatten the dough with a rolling pin. Pull out the plastic wrap and score the dough with a knife to make dents.

3. Bake in the oven for 15 minutes. Remove, cool, and break into individual crackers.

Nutrition:

- 96 calories

- 14g fat

- 4g protein

64. Spinach Soup

Preparation Time: 10 minutes

Cooking Time: 15 minutes

Servings: 8

Ingredients:

- 2 tbsp. Butter
- 20 oz. Spinach
- 1 tsp. Garlic
- Salt and ground black pepper to taste
- 45 oz. Chicken stock
- ½ tsp. Ground nutmeg
- 2 cups Heavy cream
- 1 Onion, chopped

Kitchen Equipment:

- Saucepan

Directions:

1. Heat a saucepan and melt the butter. Add onion, and stir-fry for 4 minutes. Add garlic, and stir-fry for 1 minute. Add spinach and stock, and stir-fry for 5 minutes. Remove from heat.

2. Blend soup with a hand mixer and heat the soup again. Add salt, pepper, and nutmeg, cream, stir, and cook for 5 minutes. Serve.

Nutrition:

- 158 calories
- 14.7g fat
- 3.3g protein

65. Radish Hash Browns

Preparation Time: 10 minutes

Cooking Time: 10 minutes

Servings: 4

Ingredients:

- ½ tsp. Onion powder

- 1 lb. Radishes, shredded

- ½ tsp. Garlic powder

- Salt and ground black pepper to taste

- 4 Eggs

- 1/3 cup Parmesan cheese, grated

Kitchen Equipment:

- Baking sheet

- Oven

Directions:

1. In a bowl, combine radishes, with salt, pepper, onion, garlic powder, eggs, Parmesan cheese, and mix well. Arrange on a lined baking sheet. Put in an oven at 375F and bake for 10 minutes. Serve.

Nutrition:

- 104 calories

- 6g fat

- 8.6g protein

66. Pumpkin Muffins

Preparation Time: 10 minutes

Cooking Time: 15 minutes

Servings: 18

Ingredients:

- ¼ cup sunflower seed butter
- ¾ cup pumpkin puree
- 2 tbsp. flaxseed meal
- ¼ cup coconut flour
- ½ cup erythritol
- ½ tsp. nutmeg, ground
- 1 tsp. cinnamon, ground
- ½ tsp. baking soda
- ½ tsp. baking powder
- 1 egg
- A pinch of salt

Kitchen Equipment:

- Oven
- Muffin pan

Directions:

1. In a bowl, combine butter with pumpkin puree and egg and blend well. Stir in flax-seed meal, coconut flour, erythritol, baking soda, baking powder, nutmeg, cinnamon and a pinch of salt and stir well.

2. Transfer this into a greased muffin pan, put in the oven at 350 F, and bake for 15 minutes. Set aside the muffins to cool down and serve them as a snack. Enjoy!

Nutrition:

- 65 calories
- 2.82g protein
- 5.42g fat

67. Loaded Baked Cauliflower

Preparation Time: 10 minutes

Cooking Time: 30 minutes

Servings: 2

Ingredients:

- 4 oz bacon

- 1 lb. cauliflower

- 2/3 cup sour cream

- ½ lb. cheddar cheese, shredded

- 2 tbsp. chives, finely chopped

- 1 tsp. garlic powder

- Sea salt

- Freshly ground pepper

Kitchen Equipment:

- Oven

Directions:

1. Preheat oven to 350 F. Cut the bacon into small pieces. Cook until crispy. Set aside the fat for serving. Break the cauliflower into florets. Boil until soft in lightly salted water. Drain completely.

2. Chop the cauliflower roughly. Add sour cream and garlic powder. Combine well with ¾ of the cheese and most of the finely chopped chives. Season it.

3. Put in a baking dish and top with the rest of the cheese. Bake in the oven for 10 – 15 minutes or until the cheese has melted. Top with the bacon, the rest of the chives and the bacon fat. Enjoy.

Nutrition:

- 1014 calories

- 40g protein

- 86g fat

68. Crabmeat Egg Scramble with White Sauce

Preparation Time: 10 minutes

Cooking Time: 15 minutes

Servings: 2

Ingredients:

- 1 tbsp. olive oil
- 4 eggs
- 4 oz. crabmeat
- Salt and black pepper to taste

Sauce:

- ¾ cup crème fraiche
- ½ cup chives, chopped

- ½ tsp. garlic powder
- Salt to taste

Kitchen Equipment:

- Bowl
- sauté pan

Directions:

1. Whip the eggs in a bowl using a fork, and season with salt and black pepper.

2. Set a sauté pan over medium heat and warm olive oil. Add in the eggs and scramble them.

3. Stir in crabmeat and cook until cooked thoroughly. In a mixing dish, combine crème fraiche and garlic powder. Season with salt and sprinkle with chives. Serve the eggs with the white sauce.

Nutrition:

- 105 calories
- 9g fat
- 31g protein

69. Mackerel Lettuce Cups

Preparation Time: 10 minutes

Cooking Time: 20 minutes

Servings: 4

Ingredients:

- 2 mackerel fillets, cut into pieces

- 1 tbsp. olive oil

- Salt and black pepper to taste

- 2 eggs

- 1 ½ cups water

- 1 tomato, seeded, chopped

- 2 tbsp. mayonnaise

- ½ head green lettuce, firm leaves removed for cu

Kitchen Equipment:

- Grill pan

- Pot

- Salad bowl

Directions:

1. Preheat a grill pan over medium heat. Grease the mackerel fillets with olive oil, and season well. Add the fish to the pre-heated grill pan and cook on both sides for 6-8 minutes.

2. Bring the eggs to boil in salted water in a pot over medium heat for 10 minutes. Then, run the eggs in cold water, peel, and chop into small pieces. Transfer to a salad bowl.

3. Remove the mackerel fillets to the salad bowl. Include the tomatoes and mayonnaise; mix evenly with a spoon. Layer two lettuce leaves each as cups anith two tbsp. egg salad each.

Nutrition:

- 107 calories

- 14g fat

- 27g protein

70. Watercress & Shrimp Salad with Lemon Dressing

Preparation Time: 10 minutes

Cooking Time: 1 hour 10 minutes

Servings: 2

Ingredients:

- 1 cup watercress leaves
- 2 tbsp. capers
- ½ lb. shrimp, cooked
- 1 tbsp. dill, chopped

Dressing:

- ¼ cup mayonnaise
- ½ tsp. apple cider vinegar
- ¼ tsp. sesame seeds
- Salt and black pepper to taste
- 1 tbsp. lemon juice
- 2 tsp. stevia

Kitchen Equipment:

- Large bowl

Directions:

1. Combine the watercress leaves, shrimp, and dill in a large bowl. Whisk together the mayonnaise, vinegar, sesame seeds, black pepper, stevia, and lemon juice in another bowl. Season with salt.

2. Pour some dressing over and toss it well; refrigerate for 1 hour. Top with capers to serve.

Nutrition:

- **101 calories - 8g fat - 21g protein**

71. Chicken Salad with Guacamole and Cajun Sauce

Preparation Time: 15 minutes

Cooking Time: 15 minutes

Servings: 2

Ingredients:

Cajun Spice Blend:

- 4 tsp. sweet paprika powder

- 3 tbsp.

- 1 dried thyme

- 2 cloves of garlic, minced

- 1 pinch cayenne pepper

- 1 tbsp. l. olive oil

- 450 g skinless chicken breast

- 200 g sugar peas

- 4 tomatoes

- 3 tbsp. l. olive oil

- Salt and ground black pepper

- 1 avocado

- 1 lime, juice

- 50 g arugula salad

Kitchen Equipment:

- Bowl

- saucepan

Directions:

1. In a bowl, prepare the Cajun spice mixture. Combine paprika, thyme, garlic, cayenne pepper and olive oil. Cut the chicken into long strips. Add it to a bowl and sprinkle with the spicy mixture. Leave the chicken to marinate for at least 5 minutes. Pour water into a saucepan, bring water to a boil. Add peas and cook until al dente.

2. Divide the tomatoes into quarters and remove the core and seeds. Cut the tomatoes into thin strips. Save the pulp for the vinaigrette dressing. Make a French vinaigrette dressing with tomato pulp, 2: 3 volumes of olive oil, and salt and pepper.

3. Peel the avocado; Put the pulp in a bowl and add the lime juice. Season with salt and pepper and then mashed the avocado.

4. In a skillet over medium heat, fry the chicken in olive oil for 10 to 15 minutes, until tender. Place the tomatoes and peas on the plates, sprinkle with arugula. Divide the guacamole and chicken strips into several portions. Serve the vinaigrette dressing separately.

Nutrition:

- 18g fiber

- 57g protein

- 927 calories

72. Salad with Asparagus, Eggs and Bacon

Preparation Time: 15 minutes

Cooking Time: 5 minutes

Servings: 4

Ingredients:

- 450 g green asparagus, the ends must be trimmed
- 75g bacon, crispy and chopped
- 2 large eggs, boiled, peeled and halved
- 2 tbsp. l. avocado oil or olive oil
- 2 tbsp. l. red wine vinegar
- 1 tbsp. l. Dijon mustard
- 1 tbsp. l. bacon fat
- 1 garlic clove, minced
- 1 pinch of table salt
- 1 pinch red chili flakes

Kitchen Equipment:

- Large saucepan
- Small bowl

Directions:

1. Cut the asparagus into 3 to 5-centimeter pieces.

2. Bring a large saucepan of salted water to a boil. After the water starts to boil, add the asparagus and cook for 3-4 minutes. Remove the asparagus from the boiling water with a slotted spoon and place it in an ice bath to keep it warm and retain its color and consistency.

3. Mix oil, vinegar, mustard, bacon grease, garlic, salt, and chili flakes. Stir everything by hand or using a mixer.

4. Place the asparagus on a large platter. Sprinkle bacon on top and place in hard-boiled eggs. Season with the dressing you made in a small bowl. Place the rest of the sauce on the side of the same dish.

Nutrition:

- 3g fiber
- 8g protein
- 237 calories

73. Cauliflower Salad

Preparation Time: 15 minutes

Cooking Time: 25 minutes

Servings: 6

Ingredients:

Cauliflower salad:

- 700 g large cauliflower
- Salt and ground black pepper
- 125 ml water
- 150 g bacon
- 3 stalks of celery
- ½ red onion
- 2 tbsp. l. finely chopped onion feathers

Refueling:

- 350 ml mayonnaise
- ¾ Art. l. Dijon mustard
- ¾ Art. l. apple cider vinegar
- 1 pinch of salt
- 1 pinch ground black pepper

Kitchen Equipment:

- Grill
- Qluminum foil
- Bow

Directions:

Cauliflower salad:

1. Preheat your grill.

2. Cut the cauliflower into slices. Divide and place them on two separate sheets of foil in a thin layer. Season with salt and pepper.

3. Raise the edges of the foil so that it slightly covers the cauliflower. Pour 1/4 cup water each over the cauliflower foil sheet. Cover the top with another sheet of foil and wrap well, making sure no water spills out. Grill for 15-20 minutes, keeping the center out of the heat and leaving room for the bacon.

4. Place the bacon slices in a high-sided grill pan. Bake for 10-15 minutes, until crispy. Turn them over to the other side 5-7 minutes after starting to bake.

5. Chop the celery stalks into small pieces and finely chop the red onion and onion feathers.

6. Remove bacon from grill. After cooling, cut into small pieces.

7. Take out the cauliflower and unpack. Let cool completely. After cooling, place the cauliflower in a large bowl. Add bacon, celery, onion. Save some green onions for decoration.

Refueling:

8. In a bowl, combine mayonnaise, mustard, and apple cider vinegar. Season with salt and pepper. Stir until smooth.

9. Pour the dressing over the cauliflower and mix well. Top the salad with bacon and green onions.

Nutrition:

- 3g fiber

- 6g protein

- 512 calories

74. Cobb Keto Salad with Chicken and Vinaigrette Dressing

Preparation Time: 10 minutes

Cooking Time: 25 minutes

Servings: 6

Ingredients:

Salad

- 1 package (170 g) "spring mix" - different types of salad
- 6 slices of bacon
- 2 small (200g) cooked chicken breasts, chopped
- 3 large hard-boiled eggs, chopped
- 1 medium avocado, chopped
- 1/3 cups minced green onions
- ½ cup shredded blue cheese
- 1 cup cherry tomatoes, finely chopped

Vinaigrette dressing

- 1/3 cup olive oil
- 0.25 cup wine vinegar
- 1/2 tbsp. Dijon mustard
- ½ tbsp. sugar substitute
- Salt and pepper, to taste

Kitchen Equipment:

- Large bowl

Directions:

1. Incorporate the salad ingredients in a large bowl. In a small bowl, stir the vinaigrette ingredients until the sugar substitute is completely dissolved.

2. Season the salad and it's ready to serve.

Nutrition:

- 344.12 calories
- 26.27g fat
- 21.12g protein.

75. Carrot Cake

Preparation Time: 10 minutes

Cooking Time: 35 minutes

Servings: 16

Ingredients:

- 2 eggs
- ½ tsp. vanilla
- 2 tbsp. butter, melted
- ½ cup carrots, grated
- 1/8 tsp. ground cloves
- 1 tsp. cinnamon
- 1 tsp. baking powder
- 2 tbsp. unsweetened shredded coconut
- ¼ cup pecans, chopped
- 6 tbsp. erythritol
- ¾ cup almond flour
- Pinch of salt

Kitchen Equipment:

- Oven
- Cake pan

Directions:

1. Start oven and preheat to 325 F/ 162 C. Spray cake pan with cooking spray and set aside. Whisk cloves, cinnamon, baking powder, almond flour, shredded coconut, nuts, sweetener, and salt.

2. Stir in eggs, vanilla, butter, and shredded coconut until well combined. Bake for 30-35 minutes. Slice and serve.

Nutrition:

- 111 calories
- 10.6g fat
- 1.6g fiber

6. Recipes from Spain

76. Perfect Cucumber Salsa

Preparation Time: 5 minutes

Cooking Time: 5 minutes

Servings: 10

Ingredients:

- 2 ½ cups cucumbers, peeled, seeded, and chopped
- 2 tsp. fresh cilantro, chopped
- 2 tsp. fresh parsley, chopped
- 1 ½ tbsp. fresh lemon juice
- 1 garlic clove, minced
- 1 small onion, chopped
- 2 large jalapeno peppers, chopped
- 1 ½ cups tomatoes, chopped
- ½ tsp. salt

Kitchen Equipment:

- Mixing bowl

Directions:

1. Mix all ingredients into the large mixing bowl until well combined.

2. Serve and enjoy.

Nutrition:

- 14 calories
- 0.2g fat
- 0.6g protein

77. Eggplant Chips

Preparation Time: 10 minutes

Cooking Time: 20 minutes

Servings: 15

Ingredients:

- 1 large eggplant, thinly sliced
- ¼ cup Parmesan cheese, grated
- 1 tsp. dried oregano
- ¼ tsp. dried basil
- ½ tsp. garlic powder
- ¼ cup olive oil
- ¼ tsp. pepper
- ½ tsp. salt

Kitchen Equipment:

- Oven
- Small bowl

Directions:

1. Preheat the oven to 325 F. In a small bowl, mix together oil and dried spices. Coat eggplant with oil and spice mixture and arrange eggplant slices on a baking tray.

2. Bake in a preheated oven for 15-20 minutes. Turn halfway through. Take it out from the oven and sprinkle with grated cheese. Serve and enjoy.

Nutrition:

- 77 calories
- 5.8g fat
- 3.5g protein

78. Lemon Chicken

Preparation Time: 10 minutes

Cooking Time: 45 minutes

Servings: 8

Ingredients:

- 8 chicken breasts, skinless and boneless
- 1/4 cup fresh lemon juice
- 2 tbsp. green onion, chopped
- 1 tbsp. oregano leaves
- 3 oz. feta cheese, crumbled
- 1/4 tsp. pepper

Kitchen Equipment:

- Oven
- Baking dish

Directions:

1. Prepare the oven to 350 F. Spray baking dish with cooking spray. Place chicken breasts in prepared baking dish. Drizzle with 2 tbsp. lemon juice and sprinkle with 1/2 tbsp. oregano and pepper.

2. Top with green onion and crumbled cheese. Drizzle with remaining lemon juice and oregano. Bake for 45 minutes. Serve and enjoy.

Nutrition:

- 245 calories
- 10.8g fat
- 34g protein

79. Spinach Meatballs

Preparation Time: 20 minutes

Cooking Time: 30 minutes

Servings: 4

Ingredients:

- 1 cup spinach, chopped
- 1 ½ lb. ground turkey breast
- 1 onion, chopped
- 3 cloves garlic, minced
- 1 egg, beaten
- ¼ cup milk
- ¾ cup breadcrumbs
- ½ cup Parmesan cheese, grated
- Salt and pepper to taste
- 2 tbsp. butter
- 2 tbsp. Keto flour
- 10 oz. Italian cheese, shredded
- ½ tsp. nutmeg, freshly grated
- ¼ cup parsley, chopped

Kitchen Equipment:

- Oven

Directions:

1. Set the oven at 400 F. Mix all the ingredients in a large bowl. Form meatballs from the mixture. Bake in the oven for 20 minutes.

Nutrition:

- 374 calories
- 18.5g fat
- 34.2g protein

80. Low Carb Beef Stir Fry

Preparation Time: 10 minutes

Cooking Time: 25 minutes

Servings: 3

Ingredients:

- ½ cup zucchini, spiral them into noodles about 6-inches each

- ¼ cup organic broccoli florets

- 1 bunch baby book choy, stem chopped

- 2 tbsp. avocado oil

- 2 tsp. coconut amines

- 1 small know of ginger, peeled, and cut

- 8 oz. skirt steak, thinly sliced into strips

Kitchen Equipment:

- Pan

Directions:

1. Heat the pan and add 1 tbsp. oil. Sear the steak on it on high heat. This should only take around 2 minutes per side.

2. Reduce the heat to medium and put in the broccoli, ginger, ghee, and coconut amines. Cook for a minute, stirring as often as possible.

3. Add in the book choy and cook for another minute

4. Finally, put the zucchini into the mix and cook. Note that zucchini noodles cook quickly, so you would want to pay close attention to this.

Nutrition:

- 104 calories6g fat

- 31g protein

81. Crispy Peanut Tofu and Cauliflower Rice Stir-Fry

Preparation Time: 10 minutes

Cooking Time: 80 minutes

Servings: 4

Ingredients:

- 12 oz. tofu, extra-firm
- 1 tbsp. toasted sesame oil
- 2 cloves minced garlic
- 1 small cauliflower head
- For the sauce:
- 1 ½ tbsp. toasted sesame oil
- ½ tsp. chili garlic sauce
- 2 ½ tbsp. peanut butter
- ¼ cup low sodium soy sauce
- ½ cup light brown sugar

Kitchen Equipment:

- Oven
- Skillet

Directions:

1. Start by draining the tofu for 90 minutes before getting the meal ready. You can dry the tofu quickly by rolling it on an absorbent towel and putting something heavy on top. This will create a gentle pressure on the tofu to drain out the water.

2. Preheat the oven to 400 F. While the oven heats up, cube the tofu and prepare your baking sheet.

3. Bake for 25 minutes and allow it to cool.

4. Combine the sauce ingredients and whisk it thoroughly until you get that well-blended texture. You can add more ingredients, depending on your personal preferences with taste.

5. Put the tofu in the sauce and stir it quickly to coat the tofu thoroughly. Leave it there for 15 minutes or more for a thorough marinate.

6. While the tofu marinates, shred the cauliflower into rice- size bits. You can also try buying cauliflower rice from the store to save yourself this step. Use fine grater or a food processor if ricing it manually.

7. Place skillet over medium heat. Start cooking the veggies on a bit of sesame oil and just a little bit of soy sauce. Set it aside.

8. Grab the tofu and put it on the pan. Stir the tofu frequently until it gets that nice golden-brown color. Do not worry if some of the tofu sticks to the pan – it will do that sometimes. Set aside.

9. Steam your cauliflower rice for 5 to 8 minutes. Add some sauce and stir thoroughly.

10. Now it is time to add up the ingredients together. Put the cauliflower rice with the veggies and tofu. Serve and enjoy. You can reheat this if there are leftovers but try not to leave it in the fridge for long.

Nutrition:

- 107 calories
- 9g fat
- 30g protein

82. Baked Lamb Ribs Macadamia with Tomato Salsa

Preparation Time: 10 minutes

Cooking Time: 45 minutes

Servings: 5

Ingredients:

- ½ lb. of fresh lamb ribs
- ½ cup of cherry tomatoes
- ½ tsp. pepper
- ½ cup of macadamia
- ½ tbsp. macadamia oil
- ¼ cup fresh parsley
- 1 tsp. balsamic vinegar
- 1 tsp. minced garlic
- 2 tbsp. extra virgin olive oil

Kitchen Equipment:

- Oven
- Aluminum foil
- Food processor

Directions:

1. Cut up the lamb ribs into strips or pieces
2. Preheat your oven to 204°C. Ensure that your baking tray is lined with aluminum foil.
3. Place the macadamia, garlic, parsley, pepper, and olive oil, in the food processor. Blend till the mixture is smooth and lump-free.
4. Rub your processed mixture all over your cut lamb pieces. Ensure that it is coated well enough.
5. Arrange your strips nicely in the baking tray and bake for 20-25 minutes.
6. While the lamb bakes, cut the cherry in pieces. You can cut each into four then place them in an aluminum cup.
7. Pour macadamia oil on the tomatoes. Use spoon to mix the oil and tomatoes without squishing it. The aim is to get the oil all over it. Take out your lamp and place on a plate. Place your tomatoes in the oven for 4-5 minutes.
8. Take out the tomatoes and pour sparse amounts of balsamic vinegar and stir. Pour the tomatoes on the lamb and serve warm.

Nutrition:

- 98 calories
- 7g fat
- 29g protein

83. Enticing Chicken and Broccoli Casserole

Preparation Time: 10 minutes

Cooking Time: 65 minutes

Servings: 4

Ingredients:

- 1 lb. broccoli florets

- 3 boneless, skinless chicken breasts

- 3 cups cheddar cheese, shredded or finely grated

- 1 cup of homemade zero-sugar mayonnaise

- 2 tbsp. coconut oil, melted

- ½ tsp. freshly cracked black pepper

- 1/3 cup homemade low-sodium chicken stock

- ½ tsp. sea salt

- 2 tbsp. freshly squeezed lemon juice

Kitchen Equipment:

- Oven

- Baking dish

- Aluminum foil

Directions:

1. Preheat your oven to 350 F. Brush baking dish with the coconut oil. Place the chicken pieces to the bottom of the baking dish. Spread the broccoli florets on top of the chicken. Spread half of the shredded cheddar cheese over the broccoli.

2. In a bowl, add the mayonnaise, chicken stock, sea salt, freshly cracked black pepper, and lemon juice. Pour this mixture over the chicken.

3. Sprinkle the remaining cheddar cheese over the baking dish and tightly cover the aluminum foil. Place the baking dish inside your oven and bake for 30 minutes.

4. Once done, remove the baking dish from your oven and carefully remove the aluminum foil. Return the baking dish to your oven and bake for 20 minutes. Serve and enjoy!

Nutrition:

- 107 calories

- 6g fat

- 28g protein

84. Sausage and Cheese Dip

Preparation Time: 10 minutes

Cooking Time: 80 minutes

Servings: 28

Ingredients:

- 8 oz cream cheese

- A pinch of salt and black pepper

- 16 oz sour cream

- 8 oz pepper jack cheese, chopped

- 15 oz canned tomatoes mixed with habaneros

- 1 lb. Italian sausage, ground

- ¼ cup green onions, chopped

Kitchen Equipment:

- Pan

Directions:

1. Preheat pan over medium heat, stir in sausage, and cook until it browns. Add tomatoes mix, stir and cook for 4 minutes more.

2. Season it and mix the green onions, stir and cook for 4 minutes. Spread pepper jack cheese on the bottom of your slow cooker.

3. Add cream cheese, sausage mix and sour cream, cover and cook on High for 2 hours. Uncover your slow cooker, stir dip, transfer to a bowl and serve. Enjoy!

Nutrition:

- 132 calories

- 6.79g protein

- 9.58g fat

85. Alfalfa Sprouts Salad

Preparation Time: 10 minutes

Cooking Time: 10 minutes

Servings: 4

Ingredients:

- 1 ½ tsp. Dark sesame oil

- 4 cups Alfalfa sprouts

- Salt and ground black pepper to taste

- 1 ½ tsp. Grapeseed oil

- ¼ cup Coconut yogurt

Kitchen Equipment:

- Bowl

Directions:

1. In a bowl, mix sprouts with yogurt, grape seed oil, sesame oil, salt, and pepper. Toss to coat and serve.

Nutrition:

- 83 calories

- 7.6g fat

- 1.6g protein

86. Convenient Tilapia Casserole

Preparation Time: 15 minutes

Cooking Time: 14 minutes

Servings: 4

Ingredients:

- 2 (14-oz.) cans sugar-free diced tomatoes with basil and garlic with juice

- 1/3 C. fresh parsley, chopped and divided

- ¼ tsp. dried oregano

- ½ tsp. red pepper flakes, crushed

- 4 (6-oz.) tilapia fillets

- 2 tbsp. fresh lemon juice

- 2/3 C. feta cheese, crumbled

Kitchen Equipment:

- Oven

- Shallow baking dish

Directions:

1. Preheat the oven to 4000 F. In a baking dish, stir in the tomatoes, ¼ C. of the parsley, oregano and red pepper flakes and mix until well combined.

2. Arrange the tilapia fillets over the tomato mixture in a single layer and drizzle with the lemon juice.

3. Place some tomato mixture over the tilapia fillets and sprinkle with the feta cheese evenly. Bake for about 12-14 minutes. Serve hot with the garnishing of remaining parsley.

Nutrition:

- 246 calories

- 9.4g Carbohydrates - 37.2g protein

87. Quick Dinner Tilapia

Preparation Time: 15 minutes

Cooking Time: 6 minutes

Servings: 5

Ingredients:

- 2 tbsp. coconut oil

- 5 (5-oz.) tilapia fillets

- 2 tbsp. unsweetened coconut, shredded

- 3 garlic cloves, minced

- 1 tbsp. fresh ginger, minced

- 2 tbsp. low-sodium soy sauce

- 8 scallions, chopped

Kitchen Equipment:

- Large skillet

Directions:

1. In a large skillet, cook the coconut oil over medium heat and cook the tilapia fillets for about 2 minutes. Flip the side and stir in the coconut, garlic and ginger.

2. Cook for about 1 minute. Add the soy sauce and cook for about 1 minute. Add the scallions and cook for about 1-2 more minutes. Remove from heat and serve hot.

Nutrition:

- 189 calories

- 4.4g carbohydrates

- 27.7g protein

88. Stuffed Pepper Soup

Preparation Time: 10 minutes

Cooking Time: 35 minutes

Servings: 6

Ingredients:

- 1 lb. ground beef
- 2 tbsp. coconut oil
- 1 small onion, finely chopped
- 2 large red bell peppers, seeds removed and chopped
- 1 (28-ounce) can diced tomatoes
- (14.5-ounce) can of tomato sauce
- 2 cups of homemade low-sodium chicken stock
- 2 cups of cauliflower rice
- 1 tsp. garlic powder
- 1 tsp. fine sea salt
- 1 tsp. freshly cracked black pepper

Kitchen Equipment:

- Instant pot

Directions:

1. Press the "Sauté" function on your Instant Pot and add the coconut oil, ground beef, bell peppers, and onions. Cook until the meat has browned and vegetables have softened, stirring frequently.

2. Add the remaining ingredients and stir until well combined. Close the lid and cook at high pressure for 15 minutes. When done, release the pressure and slowly take off the lid.

3. Stir the soup again and adjust the seasoning if necessary. Serve and enjoy!

Nutrition:

- 304 calories
- 10g fat
- 38g protein

89. Chicken Avocado Soup

Preparation Time: 10 minutes

Cooking Time: 20 minutes

Servings: 4

Ingredients:

- 2 lb.s of boneless, skinless chicken thighs

- 1 green onion, finely chopped

- 1 jalapeno pepper, seeds remove and chopped

- 4 cups of homemade low-sodium chicken stock

- 2 tbsp. extra-virgin olive oil

- 6 garlic cloves, peeled and minced

- 2 tsp. ground cumin

- ½ cup of fresh cilantro, chopped

- 2 limes, freshly squeezed juice

- large avocados, pitted, peeled and mashed

Kitchen Equipment:

- Instant pot

Directions:

1. Press the "Sauté" setting on your Instant Pot and add the olive oil. Once hot, place the chicken thighs and sear for 4 minutes per side or until brown.

2. Add in the remaining ingredients except for heavy cream and avocados. Close the lid and cook at high pressure for 8 minutes. When the cooking is done, quickly release the tension and remove the cover. Place the chicken in a cutting board and shred using two forks.

3. Use an immersion blender to blend inside your Instant Pot. Stir in the mashed avocados, heavy cream, and shredded chicken. Serve and enjoy!

Nutrition:

- 317 calories

- 18g fat

- 37g protein

90. Hot Avocado Curry with Shrimp

Preparation Time: 10 minutes

Cooking Time: 20 minutes

Servings: 2

Ingredients:

- ½ lb. of shrimp, peeled and deveined
- 2 cups of homemade low-sodium chicken stock
- 1 can(14-oz) coconut milk
- avocados, ripe, pitted, peeled and cut into quarters
- ½ tsp. cayenne pepper
- 1 tsp. fine sea salt
- 1 tbsp. freshly squeezed lime juice

Kitchen Equipment:

- Blender

Directions:

1. In a blender, add all the ingredients except for the shrimp. Blend until smooth and creamy. Pour in the mixture inside your Instant Pot along with the shrimp.

2. Close the lid. Cook at high pressure for 3 minutes. Then quickly release the tension and remove the cover. Adjust the seasoning if necessary. Serve and enjoy!

Nutrition:

- 317 calories
- 12g fat
- 38g protein

91. Cream of Red Bell Pepper Soup

Preparation Time: 10 minutes

Cooking Time: 30 minutes

Servings: 4

Ingredients:

- 2 ½ lb.s of red bell peppers
- 4 tbsp. coconut oil, melted
- 2 shallots, finely chopped
- medium garlic cloves, peeled and minced
- cups of homemade low-sodium vegetable stock
- 2 tsp. red wine vinegar
- ½ tsp. cayenne pepper
- 1 tsp. fine sea salt
- 1 tsp. freshly cracked black pepper
- ½ cup of heavy cream

Kitchen Equipment:

- Instant pot

Directions:

1. Select the "Sauté" function on Instant Pot and pour the coconut oil. Once hot, stir in the bell peppers, shallots, and garlic cloves. Sauté until softened, stirring occasionally.

2. Add the remaining ingredients except for the heavy cream.

3. Close the lid and set at high pressure for at least 3 minutes. Once done, let it quickly release the tension and carefully remove the cover. Use an immersion blender to blend the soup until smooth. Stir in the heavy cream and adjust the seasoning if necessary.

4. Serve and enjoy!

Nutrition:

- 302 calories
- 12g fat
- 39g protein

92. King-Style Roasted Bell Pepper Soup

Preparation Time: 10 minutes

Cooking Time: 25 minutes

Servings: 3

Ingredients:

- 4 red bell peppers, chopped
- 4 tbsp. olive oil
- 4 garlic cloves, minced
- 1 large red onion, chopped
- ¼ cup of finely grated Parmesan cheese
- 2 celery stalks, chopped
- 4 cups of homemade low-sodium vegetable broth
- 1 tsp. freshly cracked black pepper
- 1 cup of heavy cream
- 1 tsp. sea salt

Kitchen Equipment:

- Oven
- Large bowl

Directions:

1. Preheat your oven to 400 F. In a large bowl, add the chopped red bell peppers with 2 tbsp. olive oil. Stir until well coated together.

2. Transfer the red bell peppers to a baking sheet and place it inside your oven.

3. Bake the red bell peppers inside your oven for 8 to 10 minutes. Slowly remove from the oven. Set aside. Cook the remaining 2 tbsp. olive oil in a large pot over medium-high heat.

4. Once hot, add the onion, garlic, and celery. Sauté for 8 minutes, stirring occasionally.

5. Add roasted red bell peppers and chicken stock. Bring to boil. Close the lid and reduce the heat to simmer. Puree soup using immersion blender. Season it well. Mix in the heavy cream and let it boil. Then, remove from the heat. Serve and sprinkle with Parmesan cheese.

Nutrition:

- 317 calories
- 14g fat
- 37g protein

93. Duck and Eggplant Casserole

Preparation Time: 10 minutes

Cooking Time: 45 minutes

Servings: 4

Ingredients:

- 1-lb. ground duck meat
- 1 ½ tbsp. ghee, melted
- 1/3 cup double cream
- 1/2-lb. eggplant, peeled and sliced
- 1 ½ cups almond flour
- Salt and black pepper, to taste
- 1/2 tsp. fennel seeds
- 1/2 tsp. oregano, dried
- 8 eggs

Kitchen Equipment:

- Pie pan
- Oven

Directions:

1. Mix the almond flour with salt, black, fennel seeds, and oregano. Fold in one egg and the melted ghee and whisk to combine well.

2. Press the crust into the bottom of a lightly-oiled pie pan. Cook the ground duck until no longer pink for about 3 minutes, stirring continuously.

3. Whisk the remaining eggs and double cream. Fold in the browned meat and stir until everything is well incorporated. Pour the mixture into the prepared crust. Top with the eggplant slices.

4. Bake for about 40 minutes. Cut into four pieces.

Nutrition:

317 calories

10g fat

36g protein

94. Roasted Salmon Salad with Sesame Oil

Preparation Time: 10 minutes

Cooking Time: 20 minutes

Servings: 6

Ingredients:

Salad:

- 1 medium lettuce, minced
- 1 medium red pepper, minced
- 1 medium yellow pepper, minced
- 2 large pieces (350 grams each) salmon fillet
- 4 tbsp. olive oil
- 2 tbsp. coconut amino acids
- 1 tsp. sesame oil
- ¼ cup green onions, chopped

Refueling:

- 4 tbsp. olive oil
- 5 tbsp. coconut amino acids
- 1 tsp. sesame oil

Kitchen Equipment:

- Skillet

Directions:

1. Cook ¾ olive oil in a skillet over medium heat. Add sesame oil, coconut oil, and liquid amino acids. Chop the salmon into smaller pieces if necessary. Place the salmon slices in the skillet and cook for 5-7 minutes.

2. Turnover, continue cooking for another 5 minutes. The pieces should be light pink to white when cut when ready. While the salmon is cooking, put the lettuce and bell peppers in a salad bowl.

3. Prepare salad dressing in a smaller bowl. Once the salmon is done, place it on top of the lettuce and pepper leaves, add the dressing, stir the salad and enjoy!

Nutrition:

- 383 calories
- 27.14g fat
- 24.3g protein

95. Low Carb Chicken Salad with Chimichurri Sauce

Preparation Time: 10 minutes

Cooking Time: 15 minutes

Servings: 5

Ingredients:

- 250 grams of various lettuce leaves
- 2 medium chicken breasts
- 2 medium avocados, diced
- ¼ cup olive oil
- 3 tbsp. red wine vinegar
- ¼ cup parsley, chopped
- 1 tbsp. oregano
- 1 tsp. chili pepper
- 1 tsp. garlic, minced

Kitchen Equipment:

- Non-stick skillet

Directions:

1. Preheat the non-stick skillet. Place the lettuce and diced avocado in a salad bowl. Cook the chicken breasts, fry them until white. Let the chicken cool.

2. In a small bowl, combine olive oil, vinegar, parsley, oregano, garlic, and chili. Cut the chicken breast into cubes. Add the chopped chicken fillet to the salad and season with the classic chimichurri sauce.

3. Garnish the salad with additional chimichurri sauce and serve.

Nutrition:

- 285.94 calories
- 21.24 g fat — 17.24 g protein.

96. Potluck Lamb Salad

Preparation Time: 20 minutes

Cooking Time: 10 minutes

Servings: 4

Ingredients:

- 2 tbsp. olive oil, divided

- 12 oz. grass-fed lamb leg steaks, trimmed

- Salt and black pepper, to taste

- 6½ oz. halloumi cheese, cut into thick slices

- 2 jarred roasted red bell peppers, sliced thinly

- 2 cucumbers, cut into thin ribbons

- 3 C. fresh baby spinach

- 2 tbsp. balsamic vinegar

Kitchen Equipment:

- Skillet

Directions:

1. In a skillet, heat 1 tbsp. the oil over medium-high heat and cook the lamb steaks for about 4-5 minutes per side or until desired doneness. Transfer the lamb steaks onto a cutting board for about 5 minutes. Then cut the lamb steaks into thin slices. In the same skillet, add halloumi and cook for about 1-2 minutes per side or until golden.

2. In a salad bowl, add the lamb, halloumi, bell pepper, cucumber, salad leaves, vinegar, and remaining oil and toss to combine.

3. Serve immediately.

Nutrition:

- 420 calories

- 35.4g protein — 1.3g fiber.

97. Spring Supper Salad

Preparation Time: 15 minutes

Cooking Time: 5 minutes

Servings: 5

Ingredients:

For Salad:

- 1 lb. fresh asparagus

- ½ lb. smoked salmon, cut into bite-sized pieces

- 2 heads red leaf lettuce, torn

- ¼ C. pecans, toasted and chopped

For Dressing:

- ¼ C. olive oil

- 2 tbsp. fresh lemon juice

- 1 tsp. Dijon mustard

- Salt and black pepper, to taste

Kitchen Equipment:

- Pan

Directions:

1. In a boiling water, stir in the asparagus and cook for about 5 minutes. Drain the asparagus well. In a serving bowl, add the asparagus and remaining salad ingredients and mix.

2. In another bowl, add all the dressing ingredients and beat until well combined. Place the dressing over salad and gently toss to coat well. Serve immediately.

Nutrition:

- 223 calories

- 8.5g Carbohydrates — 3.5g fiber.

98. Chicken-of-Sea Salad

Preparation Time: 15 minutes

Cooking Time: 5 minutes

Servings: 6

Ingredients:

- 2 (6-oz.) cans olive oil-packed tuna, drained
- 2 (6-oz.) cans water packed tuna, drained
- ¾ C. mayonnaise
- 2 celery stalks, chopped
- ¼ of onion, chopped
- 1 tbsp. fresh lime juice
- 2 tbsp. mustard
- Freshly ground black pepper, to taste
- 6 C. fresh baby arugula

Kitchen Equipment:

- Large bowl

Directions:

1. In a large bowl, incorporate all the ingredients except arugula and gently stir to combine. Divide arugula onto serving plates and top with tuna mixture. Serve immediately.

Nutrition:

- 325 calories
- 27.4g protein
- 1.1g fiber

99. Keto Kohlrabi Salad

Preparation Time: 10 minutes

Cooking Time: 0 minute

Servings: 2

Ingredients:

- 450g kohlrabi
- 225ml plain mayonnaise or vegan mayonnaise
- Salt and pepper
- Fresh parsley (optional)

Kitchen Equipment:

- Bowl

Directions:

1. Clean the kohlrabi. Be sure to cut out any tough parts of the cabbage. Slice, chop, or chop and place in a bowl. Add mayonnaise to the cabbage and, if desired, fresh herbs. Season the kohlrabi salad with salt and pepper to taste.

Nutrition:

- 4g fiber
- 41g fat
- 405 calories

100. Coconut Cake

Preparation Time: 10 minutes

Cooking Time: 20 minutes

Servings: 8

Ingredients: parated

- ½ tsp. baking powder
- 5 eggs, se
- ½ tsp. vanilla
- ½ cup butter softened
- ½ cup erythritol
- ¼ cup unsweetened coconut milk
- ½ cup coconut flour
- Pinch of salt

Kitchen Equipment:

- Oven
- Cake pan

Directions:

1. Start to preheat oven to 400 F/ 200 C. Grease cake pan with butter and set aside. In a bowl, beat sweetener and butter until combined. Add egg yolks, coconut milk, and vanilla and mix well.

2. Add baking powder, coconut flour, and salt and stir well. In another bowl, beat egg whites until stiff peak forms. Combine the egg whites into the cake mixture.

3. Pour batter in a prepared cake pan and bake in preheated oven for 20 minutes. Slice and serve.

Nutrition:

- 163 calories
- 16.2g fat — 3.9g protein

CPSIA information can be obtained
at www.ICGtesting.com
Printed in the USA
BVHW011406170921
616898BV00021B/209